protecting your church against

sexual
predators

protecting your church against

sexual predators

Voyle A. Glover, Esq.

Kregel
Academic & Professional

Protecting Your Church Against Sexual Predators: Legal FAQs for Church Leaders

© 2005 by Voyle A. Glover

Published in 2005 by Kregel Publications, a division of Kregel, Inc., P.O. Box 2607, Grand Rapids, MI 49501.

This book is designed to provide information of a general nature and as a survey of issues, not as a legal guide. As such, it is not a substitute for legal counsel, and readers must consult with an attorney to determine specific federal, state, or local statutes that may apply in their individual communities or to their organizations in order to formulate policies or take any actions related to the subjects discussed herein.

All Scripture quotations, unless otherwise indicated, are from the King James Version of the Bible.

Scripture quotations marked NKJV are taken from the New King James Version. Copyright © 1982 by Thomas Nelson, Inc. Used by permission. All rights reserved.

Library of Congress Cataloging-in-Publication Data
Glover, Voyle A.
    Protecting your church against sexual predators: legal FAQs for church leaders / by Voyle A. Glover.
    p.   cm.
    Includes bibliographical references.
    1. Child sexual abuse—United States. 2. Church employees—Legal status, laws, etc.—United States. 3. Clergy—Malpractice—United States. I. Title.
KF9323.Z9G58 2005   345.73'02536--dc22   2005010884

ISBN 0-8254-2691-X

Printed in the United States of America

07 08 09 / 5 4 3 2

Contents

Preface

S exual predators within our congregations have dramatically increased the legal liability for Christian churches. Children and teens are sexually assaulted within the church. This is a matter of primary concern to every church member and particularly to every church leader. Child molesters sit in our pews. They come to our picnics. They may even teach. We have been infiltrated, and we'd better wake up and take necessary protection measures.

Some sexual predators are church members. But more prominent and deadly are those who prey on children through their roles as pastors, music leaders, youth directors, and counselors. Research suggests that more cases of sexual misconduct involve ordained and other professional staff than involve volunteer workers. The greatest financial damages against churches have resulted from unlawful sexual assaults by those in professional ministry.

Churches must insist on accountability from their leaders.

Leaders must insist on being accountable, even if the congregation does not make such a demand.

Everyone who comes into contact with children and teens, whatever the occasion, must insist on strong accountability from everyone, from leaders to fill-in volunteers. No congregation should ignore this mandate.

Churches today live in a context in which there has been a groundswell of litigation. Roman Catholics, in particular, have experienced an unprecedented flood of lawsuits. Their losses are now in the billions of dollars. Around the U.S., individuals have awakened to the sudden vulnerability of the church. Some see opportunity. They make claims that have no merit with the hope of profiting. Others have truly been harmed and are seeking redress from the institution they perceive as being the instrument of that harm.

But there's more. Attorneys are awakening to the fact that churches can have very "deep pockets." Many lawyers have turned their attention to the churches. Seminars are now being held to teach lawyers how to try cases against churches. Briefs are traded online. Information is shared, much as it was in the huge tobacco litigation.

There is little question but that the churches in America have become a target.

To protect the church from sexual predators requires the attention of pastors, elders, deacons, and other ministry leaders whose interests and expertise do not run toward legal matters. Now they must turn their attention to such administrative matters as screening prospective employees and volunteers.

Church leaders face a human resources task akin to that of the modern corporate executive, but they lack the resources and expertise available in most corporations. A corporation, for example, will have a human resources individual and perhaps even staff who are trained to deal with state and federal rules and regulations. People are at hand who know the laws governing employee relations, hiring practices, and labor practices. Only some megachurches have such resources. Other congregations are fortunate if they have a lawyer who is a member and will donate consultant service. Far too many church leaders simply trust their instincts in the administration of volunteer and paid staff. That can result in disaster in today's complex legal landscape.

This book is not designed to be the definitive resource on sexual predators in the church. Much more could be said about the subjects addressed. It is tightly focused on one thing: *minimizing the legal exposure of a church.* We can't prevent every bad thing from happening, but we can show a jury that we took precautions. If it happened, it was in spite of reasonable efforts. This won't take away all the pain, but it may enable us to dodge the proverbial "legal bullet" that otherwise might leave a church bankrupt.

Protecting our children is protecting the church itself. Like salvation and faith, one intertwines with the other. The church that cares enough to protect its children and teens will secondarily protect itself from destruction or serious harm.

I have condensed a lot of material so that we can "cut to the chase." I want church leaders to read this, and I know we're all busy people. I understand that reading a legal treatise is not at the top of most folks' list and that's why I've avoided turning this into such a thing. You'll find it's a quick read, packed with valuable information that could save lives from devastation, and also keep the corporate body of Christ from harm.

My prayer is that the information in this book will be used of God to protect churches and children from disaster.

VOYLE A. GLOVER
ATTORNEY AT LAW

1

Coming Soon to Your Church: A Child Molester

In church after church around the world, reports have come to light about children being molested by someone in the place where they should feel safest. The Roman Catholic Church is reeling from staggering financial judgments in lawsuits filed by molestation victims. Most of these cases have come into the spotlight many years after the alleged sexual crimes occurred. For decades, the Catholic Church quietly settled abuse cases out of court and shuffled pedophile priests to different parishes. Not until the early 1980s did the news media start digging into allegations that had surfaced in places such as New Orleans, Louisiana.[1] In 1992, the Boston scandals began a nightmare of litigation for Roman Catholic diocese administrators in the United States. After more than a decade, the end of litigation is not yet in sight.

But the Roman Catholic Church is only the most visible defendant. Lawyers also have other church organizations in their sights. In some of the targeted churches, leaders have made the same mistakes that got the Roman Catholic bishops into so much trouble. Incidents were concealed. Law enforcement agencies were stonewalled. Safeguards were lacking. Misconduct was not subjected to church discipline.

Sexual misconduct toward children in the church is not new, but attitudes and perspectives about child molesters have changed and absolutely must change. Otherwise we will continue to cope with devastated lives, financial disaster, and member disillusionment. Church leaders had better take a long, hard look at this issue.

To begin with, let us look at some facts about these crimes:

1. The vast majority of child molesters are male.[2]
2. Victims may be male or female.
3. Child molesters tend to work hard to win positions of trust. Authority, trust, and respect enable molesters to manipulate children, parents, and other leaders.
4. A child molester will create fear in the child, so that the child is afraid to tell anyone.
5. There are no "typical" child molesters. They may be of any age.
6. A child molester in the church looks for and tries to create opportunities to be alone with a child or children.
7. Prior to being caught, the typical child molester attacks thirteen children.
8. Child molesters often are married, may show evidence of a strong Christian witness, and may be in positions of responsibility.[3]
9. Child molesters often do not recognize that any harm has come to their victims. Frequently, there is more remorse from being caught than for injuries inflicted by the crime.
10. A child molester is very likely to return to criminal sexual behavior after release from prison.[4]

FAQ   Why should I expect a child molester to come into my congregation?

ANSWER   *Churches provide one of the best sources for children to be found. An atmosphere of trust and acceptance makes the church one of the easiest places for predators to find opportunities to attack victims.*

Child Abuse Statistics on the Rise

Since the 1970s, child abuse is far more likely to be reported than it was before. In California, for example, the number of reports investigated rose from about 119,000 in 1976 to about 475,000 in 1988.[5] A similar statistical increase occurred throughout the United States and Canada. In 1976, fewer than 6,000 incidents of a sexual nature involving children were reported to law enforcement and child welfare workers. Once sexual abuse became more widely recognized and reporting was encouraged, the number of reports increased to 130,000 in 1986. The number tripled between 1980 and 1986 alone. Today, more than 300,000 child sexual abuse reports are investigated annually in the United States.[6]

So, whereas the church might have been forgiven for being caught unawares by pedophiles in the 1970s, there is no excuse today. Ample warning has been given. The church is a natural magnet for children. Pedophiles hunt children. Thus, it would be foolish to think that pedophile child molesters wouldn't regard the church as a hunting ground. However, in an interview with *Christianity Today*, attorney Richard Hammar, an author and expert in legal aspects of church life, said, "Our research indicates that 70 percent of churches are doing absolutely nothing to screen volunteer youth workers."[7]

Molesters May Assault Many

There are no "absolute" statistics on the number of children molested every day in the United States, Canada, or any other country. Despite the increased awareness of the problem, and the likelihood that a sexual incident will be reported, many still go unreported. In some nations, molestation is not discussed as freely as it is in North America. We can only trace numbers of complaints, investigations, arrests, convictions, and releases.[8] Research on adults who were sexually abused as children suggests that the large majority of victims do not report their abuse at the time it occurs. Children often keep their history of abuse a secret because they fear their parents' rejection, punishment, and blame.[9]

In a typical church environment, guilt and the potential stigma associated with abuse, coupled with the understanding of how homosexual acts are viewed by the church, often will silence an abused child, particularly if he or she is in or near the teenage years. Younger children are often sworn to secrecy with threats of violence or some vague, undefined "doom" that will occur. The real tragedy is that, while their little lips are sealed, so are their hearts.

Remember, the typical child molester does not wear a sign. And the victims are not clamoring to tell their stories of molestation. They are sitting in church with sad eyes, quiet, confused, and hurting.

The typical child molester has a string of prior victims and may or may not have been detected yet. He is calculating and cunning, waiting for opportunity. The only question is whether the particular church he has chosen (or that chose him) will afford him the opportunity he needs.

One attempt to estimate the number of victims in 1998 was published in the 2001 *Annual Review of Sociology.* For all kinds of violent crime in 1998, including sexual attacks, 87.9 of every thousand U.S. adolescents between the ages of twelve to fifteen became victims. A slightly higher rate of 96.2 of every thousand teens between the ages of sixteen and nineteen became victims. For people in their twenties, the chance of becoming a victim of violent crime drops rapidly. At age sixty-five, only 4.4 of every thousand persons are victims. Ross Macmillan, who wrote the report, observed that the age variables apply to all the kinds of violent crime studied. Robberies and sexual assaults were ten times as likely among adolescents. Other assaults were twenty-three times more likely.[10]

Sixty-seven percent of *all* victims of sexual assault reported to law enforcement agencies were under the age of eighteen; 34 percent of all victims were under the age of twelve. One of every seven victims of sexual assault reported to law enforcement agencies was under the age of six.[11]

Population and Pornography Increase Sex Crimes

Several reasons might be suggested for actual increases in crime numbers, as opposed to increases due to better reporting and a greater willingness to talk about behavior that might be identified as sexual. Natural increases in population certainly play a part in crime statistics. Another factor that is increasingly being blamed is the easier availability of child and adult pornography on the Internet, which may come to the attention of people who have sexual proclivities that they might not have acted upon in the past. Assuming that Internet pornography will not become more controlled and less available, we can expect that the rate of sexual assaults, including child molestation, will continue to outpace population growth. This increases the chances that our communities and our churches have pedophiles or people with pedophiliac tendencies. In short, pedophiles are all around, and some are church members.

FAQ   What does a child molester look like?

ANSWER *He looks like you, especially if you are a man.*

- Pedophiliac child molesters are invariably male. Although there are some female molesters, they are few and their victims are typically males in their teens. The American Professional Society on the Abuse of Children reports: "In both clinical and nonclinical samples, the vast majority of offenders are male."[12]
- A significant percentage of victims are males. A study undertaken by the *Journal of Sex and Marital Therapy,* of 457 male sex offenders who had committed crimes against children, found that about one-third of these sexual offenders targeted male victims.[13]
- Child molesters can be preteens or grandfathers. A U.S. Department of Justice report, titled "Criminal Offender Statistics," found that criminal offenders who had victimized a child

were on average five years older than violent offenders who had committed crimes against adults. Nearly 25 percent of child victimizers were age forty or older.[14] Forty percent of the offenders who victimized children under the age of six were juveniles under the age of eighteen—one reason to keep male teens out of the nursery.[15]

A Child Molester May Have Been a Victim

It is not uncommon for molesters to have been victimized in their own childhood. There is also evidence that the greater number of male child molesters are homosexual. Quoting *Journal of Sex Research* statistics, David Wagner, an associate law professor at Regent University School of Law, said that heterosexuals outnumber homosexuals by a ratio of at least twenty to one (in other words, homosexuals comprise about 5 percent of the population), yet homosexual pedophiles commit about one-third of all child sex offenses.[16]

FAQ   Christ forgives sinners. So if a repentant child molester comes into my church, shouldn't I treat him just as I would any other sinner?

ANSWER No! If you do that, you may one day be called to account for your failure to recognize the danger posed by such an individual. Ignorance may not be a valid defense.

In a Midwestern Baptist church, a man sat comfortably in his pew near the front with his wife nearly every Sunday. He was in his sixties and was always quick to confess his faith. He'd gone on a cross-cultural missions trip with a group from the church. His witness to coworkers was important to him, and he often would share stories of his efforts.

The man carried his Bible faithfully to church and was the most active participant in his Sunday school class. It was not uncommon for him to engage the teacher in an animated discussion of some point in the lesson, after which he always told the teacher how much he'd enjoyed the lesson.

Then one Sunday he was not in his usual place. He'd been arrested and was in the county jail, facing a charge of child molestation. He was convicted and at this writing is still serving his sentence. After release, he may return to his pew and ask to be readmitted to membership. The question is, what liability will the church face with this known sex offender?

Defining Repentance and Restoration

Even among pastors and other church leaders, there is a diversity of views about what *repentance* and *restoration* mean. Within a congregation, there are a wide range of theological and life understandings about these concepts. The pastor and congregation may not agree about how to relate to sexual offenders who seek restoration or membership.

You must recognize that repentance is not merely being sorry for one's sins. I have seen many individuals who were sorry for the wrong they had done, but there was no godly sorrow. Their sorrow was directed more toward their circumstances, or sorrow that they were caught and humiliated. The would-be conqueror of the world, Napoleon Bonaparte, gazed upon the tomb of the philosopher Jean-Jacques Rousseau, whose ideas had fueled the French Revolution. He is reported to have said: "Maybe it would have been better if neither of us had been born."[17] Godly sorrow differs from mere remorse (see 2 Cor. 7:8–11). The apostle Paul describes godly sorrow as coming from God. It is the sorrow of a soul who has turned away from the wrong and toward God. Such a heart is encompassed with sorrow for the wrong because it first of all is an offense against God.

One thing I have learned from years of dealing with people and seeing many examples of fake repentance and genuine repentance is that those whose repentance is godly are always pliable. The truly repentant are willing to accept church discipline, to accept rules, and to yield their wills. They are willing to work toward restoration without rebellion or resistance.

Restoration cannot come without godly repentance. Unfortunately, we mere mortals cannot discern it infallibly. Tears and a measure of pliability are good indications but not proof positive. The reality is that we cannot know the heart of an individual. We can only evaluate the evidence shown by a life.

As a practical matter, that means that full acceptance of someone who has fallen into egregious sin ought to take some time. We need to see good works. We need to see a godly life. We need to see fruits of repentance.

Of course, restoration is to be done by those who are spiritual: "Brethren, if a man be overtaken in a fault, ye which are spiritual, restore such an one in the spirit of meekness; considering thyself, lest thou also be tempted" (Gal. 6:1). In efforts to restore an individual to spiritual health and fellowship with God and the congregation, attention must be paid to identify (1) who will undertake the effort; and (2) what those efforts will be. The Greek word translated *restore* means "to mend; to furnish completely." Its tense is the continuous present, meaning there is an unfinished perseverance that will involve patient waiting. A church should employ a process that involves spiritual men with a planned program of restoration that is designed to ultimately achieve the results of restoring the individual to spiritual health and fellowship with God and the congregation. For some excellent resources dealing with restoration issues, see appendix F of this volume, "Resources."

One thing is certain: If your church accepts as a member a man who is a sex offender and fails to address those two issues of repentance and restoration, I assure you that the plaintiff's lawyer will raise them. Even a secular court, in sentencing a defendant, looks for repentance and remorse.

One cannot afford to fall back to a superficial conclusion of "Well, the Bible… it says we are to forgive a man. Christ died to save sinners, and we gotta give this fellow a chance and quit being suspicious of him." Be very, very careful you don't get sucked into substituting someone's well-intentioned understanding of forgiveness and love for true biblical forgiveness and love.

Responsibility is an integral part of those concepts of forgiveness and love. As a church leader, you have a responsibility to insure the safety of the flock as well as a responsibility to see to it that the congregation has a true understanding of the difference between loving the fallen sinner and loving him responsibly. You cannot put the membership at risk.

This means wisdom, discretion, and prudence must be imbedded in responses of love and forgiveness. For example, if I forgive someone for stealing my wallet, this does not mean I must now demonstrate my forgiveness by leaving my wallet available as a sign of love and trust. The Bible does not teach that I am to place unrestrained, implicit trust in that individual.

Unfortunately, that is what some churches feel they must do where a man has fallen into the sin of sexual assault. That is irresponsible and dangerous to him and to the church.

Can You Afford to Give a Guarantee?

Even if there is solid agreement in the congregation as to how the matter of a repentant sexual offender should be dealt with (which means that the people know the biblical requirements), there are also legal issues. Let's assume that there is genuine repentance, and a biblical program of restoration is instituted. No church leader will be able to guarantee that there will not be another moral failure. For that matter, leaders can't guarantee that any church member will always abide by the Christian model of behavior that they have agreed to follow in the area of their addictions and weaknesses. No church leader can make an ironclad guarantee to parents in the congregation that a repentant child molester will never molest one of their children. A smart lawyer would put the pastor or leaders on the stand and engage them as follows:

"You're the pastor in the church, sir?"

"Yes."

"Tell me, Pastor, can you explain the term *backslider?*"

"Of course. That is where a Christian sins, where he or she gets out of fellowship with the Lord and does something that is not in keeping with a Christian pattern of behavior."

"Does this happen often to Christians? I mean, is it common?"

"Some more than others. But yes, I'd say it's a common thing to have happen."

"Pastor, if a man who was once an alcoholic came into your midst, is it possible he might, well, you know, *backslide?*"

"Certainly, it is possible."

"Even if he'd previously repented of that sin of drunkenness?"

"Yes."

"Then, Pastor, you had to know the potential for your church member, Mr. Mol Ester, to backslide, didn't you?"

The pastor shifts uncomfortably, aware of where the questioning is going. "Uh, well, certainly. But we had no warnings or evidence that he was…"

"That wasn't the question, Pastor. You knew he could backslide, didn't you? Yes or no."

"Yes."

"And in spite of that, you made no effort to watch this man, no effort to keep him from the children, no effort to ensure the safety of those children placed in your care, did you?"

"Well, we did, yes, certainly."

Trust me when I say, it's all downhill from that point.

A program of restoration for a sex offender is going to vary from church to church and from denomination to denomination. But all of them ought to have, at minimum, the following features:

1. *Accountability.* There should be at least one individual to whom the person being restored is accountable. It should be male to male, female to female.

2. *Teaching.* Some teaching must be done on a mentoring/discipling basis with respect to holiness, particularly in the area of moral purity. The individual must be made aware of the biblical concepts of morality.

3. *Prayer.* There should be a group with whom this individual can meet and pray.
4. *Worship Attendance.* This individual needs a program that insures that his attendance in corporate worship is regular and faithful. It isn't that he must attend every service, or else he's given the boot. Rather he is compelled to maintain attendance as a part of the restoration process and must give account of his reasons for missing church.
5. *Integration.* The individual who is being restored needs help in the integration of himself into the congregation. Beyond attending some of the functions of the church, that means taking part in the social life as well.
6. *Duty.* Every restoration effort must include the assignment of some kind of duty or responsibility to the individual. Give him something to do, even if it is merely helping clean the church one day a week or helping in a project.

There are other excellent ideas. Whatever plan your church chooses, make sure the steps are followed faithfully. In a worst-case event, you will need to detail what efforts you made to restore this person to fellowship, and why you did what you did. Remember, the world is going to wonder why you even let this person come in. So if you're going to restore someone, make sure you know what you're doing and why you're doing it.

Accepting a Convicted Child Molester into Membership
A church that accepts a man into their midst who has a history of child molesting is at risk legally. If he comes into the congregation and one day molests a child, the church may well face a civil lawsuit filed by the parents on behalf of the child, and in some states, the parents may have their own separate legal action against the church as well.

Obviously, it is ridiculous to suggest that a church should never admit such a person into the congregation. Every person brings some sort of "past" into the church, including murderers like the apostle Paul (1 Tim. 1:12–16). This fact is one of the hallmarks of Christianity.

Christ died for sinners (Rom. 5:6–8; 1 Cor. 15:3–10; 1 Peter 3:18). We'd certainly like for all those sinners to be "like us" (and not have such a horrible past), and then we have to remember our own horrible past. The bottom line is that we're going to have people coming to the church who have a wide array of life experiences, including crimes.

I believe that Christ died for sinners, even child molesters. But I also believe that those who have committed this sin have done a crime that was so wicked that Jesus felt it would be better for them to be put to death (Matt. 18:6). We need to think about that. It would be wise (and biblical) for a church faced with such an issue to prayerfully consider what should be done.

If the offender is pliable—willing to submit to the authority of the church and undergo whatever discipline, discipleship, and other constraints are required for a period of time—then restoration to fellowship can occur. Whatever the church rules or policy, there absolutely must be some kind of a biblical restoration process prior to admitting such a person back into the fellowship. Even with a restorative process, there is always a risk with this kind of a member. If the church has done nothing at all, then it will look far worse if a case ever is filed and comes to a trial. There is an assumed responsibility to at least try to make sure that this person is fit to come within the fellowship of the congregation.

FAQ How should I treat a member who has been accused of molestation?

ANSWER Don't play lawyer, judge, or jury. If a parent comes to you with an allegation, immediately refer him or her to the civil authorities.

You can't afford to put the church in the middle. The church is not an investigative arm of the state and has neither the resources nor the skills to make a determination as to the validity of such charges. You might approach the accused in some circumstances and confront him with the accusations. However, if he confesses, it may present a problem for you, depending on the laws of your state or nation. The confession might be one that cannot be used against him in a court of law, and you may have a confession that you can't even bring before the congregation (see appendix G: "Mandatory Reporters of Child Abuse and Neglect").

There have been circumstances in which pastors have successfully confronted the accused. I know of one pastor who got a confession from a man and went with him to the police station, where he turned himself in and again confessed. But such instances are very rare. I know of another situation in which a man confessed when confronted by the pastor, but later, when confronted by the police, denied he'd confessed and threatened to sue the pastor for making a false accusation against him. A more prudent course of action is to refer the complaining parents immediately to the authorities (usually the local police department). You may wish to accompany them, as part of assisting and helping the victims.

2

Appreciating the Danger Posed by Child Molesters

FAQ   What should I know about a convicted child molester?

ANSWER   *The more you understand the nature and habits and think-ing of child molesters, the better able you will be to appre-ciate the danger they pose to your church and the children in your church.*

Understanding the Danger

There is always a danger that a book such as this, which uses strong words to make some important points, may leave church lead-ers paranoid. The aim is not to provoke irrational fear, but rather to promote a more watchful attitude. Leaders need to realize that most churches are easy targets for pedophiles. There is no way that the dynamic, interpersonal community of people we know as the church can be kept 100 percent safe from the predations of a determined pedophile. Even with every reasonable safeguard in place, there is still the possibility that your church will be hit by this vicious crime.

But churches certainly can minimize the risk.

Protecting your congregation begins with a clear appreciation of the danger posed by pedophiles, which means you must gain an understanding of them. It isn't enough to simply classify them as sinners who are guilty of not letting Christ rule in their lives. When a reformed alcoholic fails we can shrug and say that Christ was not ruling or he was not "walking in the Spirit" or is "backslidden." With sexual predators, though, the consequences of failure are too great to cover with a cliché. A backslidden child molester or sexual predator is a disaster for the entire church. It is the church's business to pay close attention to this "not so ordinary" sinner.

Lawmakers have come to understand that men who have been convicted of child molesting pose a serious threat after their release from prison. In the United States, both national and state governments have passed legislation to protect the public from convicted sex offenders.

The brutal 1994 rape and murder of seven-year-old Megan Kanka sparked a public outcry for community notification. On May 17, 1996, President Bill Clinton signed a law requiring sex offenders to register, and for communities to be notified of the release of convicted sex offenders. This federal law came to be known as Megan's Law.[1] Further, the United States Congress passed the 1994 Jacob Wetterling Act, which requires states to register individuals convicted of sex crimes against children. The privacy interests of convicted sex offenders are considered less important than the government's interest in public safety.[2]

Components of Megan's Law allow the states some discretion to establish criteria for disclosure, but all states must make private and personal information on registered sex offenders available to the public. This law, combined with prior legislation, demonstrates an increasing public awareness of the dangers posed by child molesters.[3]

There Is No Cure for Child Molesters

Throughout the legal and treatment communities, it is generally believed that a pedophile's mind-set is so corrupted that he is never regarded as cured. Supported by some research, conventional wisdom holds that male sex offenders who prey on children can be expected to repeat their crime eventually.[4] Such a viewpoint doesn't take into account Christ's ability to change a pedophile's heart and mind and make him into a new creature, but to ignore the strength of pedophilia addiction, even in changed pedophiles, is to court disaster.[5]

The conclusion that child molesters are never cured comes from interpreting data that indicates pedophiles are wired differently in their psychosexual makeup, which is at the core of human self-identity. What this means for church leaders is that a man who has molested children in the past can never again be trusted, even if he has the best intentions and shows all indications of change. It can be assumed that the temptation remains, and that it is sometimes a strong temptation.[6] David Grimm, a marriage and family therapist who has worked extensively with sex offenders and victims, stated: "It's not curable, but the best you can hope for is to engage the person's conscience so they don't want to create new victims."[7]

Indeed, the recidivism level is such that many states have taken the drastic step to implement chemical castration of some sex offenders.[8] At least one court said the danger of recidivism is great enough to require a system of registration in order to enable law enforcement officials to identify previous offenders as well as to alert the public.[9] The United States Supreme Court in *Kansas v. Hendricks,* 521 US 346 (1997), upheld an attempt by the state of Kansas to incorporate repeat sex offenders into the state's system of involuntary civil commitment, which can be applied to those who suffer from a "mental abnormality."[10]

Child Molesters Are Good at Hiding Their True Selves

A child predator who is actively seeking sexual contact with children usually is very good at hiding his true self. He will enlist the unknowing help of anyone he can. This means that a pastor who befriends a pedophile to the point of clouding his good judgment becomes an enabler who may pay the price when a lawsuit hits.

A pastor in Pennsylvania learned that lesson when he thought he was buying airplane tickets to help a young man start a new life and instead found himself facing criminal prosecution on charges of "aiding and abetting" a sex offender who was fleeing prosecution. The young man had been accused of molesting a five-year-old girl.[11] This pastor put himself and his church at risk. It was a foolish thing to do. He confused love with responsibility.

FAQ How should a church respond to a convicted child molester who desires church membership?

ANSWER *You are not God. You cannot know the heart of another human being. You do not know for certain that this man is genuinely repentant of his sin of child molesting. Even if he is, you really do not know the personal struggles he faces. Consequently, you do not know whether he can be trusted. Your response should be founded in wisdom and prudence, with an eye toward erring on the side of common sense and the protection of the children in your care.*

Some Assumptions You Must Make

If you have a convicted child molester in your congregation, you have to assume three things:

1. This sin will always be a temptation to him.
2. This man will no doubt do what all Christians do in life: *stumble, fall, fail, and exhibit weaknesses and doubts.*
3. There is a very substantial likelihood that, for this man, *stumbling* means he will commit an act that harms a child.

Although we know that all Christians fall into sin—and that "backsliding," for some, can have catastrophic results—it does not mean that church leaders must continually think the worst about someone in their congregation or assume that he is lying about his spiritual growth. It does mean that the leaders and the convicted child molester must candidly look at reality.

If the man is honest with himself and others, he should be open to guidance and accountability and agree with the need for close attention. He has already demonstrated that he is not above the crime of pedophilia. Even with counseling and the threat of punishment, he should be aware that statistically he is likely to do it again. He may not believe that he will fall into that statistical majority, but he must acknowledge the possibility. At any rate, the church must assume that he might fall back into sin.

One convicted child molester, Larry Don Mcquay, stated, "I got away with molesting over 240 children before getting caught for molesting just one little boy." He added, "With all that I have cold-heartedly learned while in prison, there is no way that I will ever be caught again. I am doomed to eventually rape, then murder, my poor little victims to keep them from telling on me." These were his words in his plea to authorities to castrate him before his scheduled release for the 1989 rape of a six-year-old boy.[12]

Ernie Allen, one of the foremost U.S. experts on child molestation, strongly defended Megan's Law from civil libertarians who argued that it conflicted with privacy rights: "The majority of the victims of America's sex offenders are kids, and research has shown that a significant subset of the sex offender population represents the highest risk of re-offense. They are coming back into our communities."[13] Concerning the recidivism rate, Allen said:

> Justice Department data indicate that six out of every ten convicted child molesters have a prior conviction, prior history. One out of every four has a history of violent sexual offenses. Forty-eight percent of convicted sex offenders in America's prisons will be arrested for a felony or serious misdemeanor within three years of their release. Of the quarter of a million sex offenders currently under the care and control of correctional agencies in the United States, sixty percent of them today are in the community, and virtually all of them are coming back to the community.[14]

A Child Molester Will Likely Be a Repeat Offender

Allen and most other researchers in the field believe it is imperative that secular communities (and presumably they would add Christian communities) become aware of those most likely to act again as sexual predators. Because of the high rate of repeat offenses, it is important for communities to know about men in their midst who have been in prison for child molestation. That is why Megan's Law was one of the most accepted major legal developments of the 1990s.

In 1966, California became the first state to enact a law providing for chemical castration of convicted sex criminals.[15] Other states soon followed. Although the treatment, using a drug called Depo Provera, has its advantages, one cold, hard fact must be considered: Once a man stops taking Depo Provera injections, his suppressed sexual urges will resurface. Side effects from the drug, while reportedly mild, are substantial enough that most men are not motivated to continue treatments after release from prison.[16] Unless treatment continues after the offender returns to the community, the "castration" is a temporary fix that arguably was meaningless because there are no child victims for the molester in prison.

A "Restored" Church Member Is Still a Risk

It seems harsh to say that a church can restore and forgive a child molester but he must always be treated with an awareness of his past criminal activity. No doubt some who read this will react negatively. Christians seek to rescue and minister to people whose lives have been mangled by sin. We do not like to think that evil still lurks in those rescued hearts. Of course we know that evil still lurks in all of our hearts, but it is the particular nature of the evil we are talking about here—for which others may bear the cost of our acceptance—that gives us pause. We don't want to walk around suspicious of fellow Christians, and we shouldn't. But we must remain forever vigilant because of the peculiar and dangerous nature of this particular sin.

Church leaders must consider as "high risk" anyone who comes into the congregation after molesting children—even if he or she has been fully restored. Acceptance must be openly accompanied by wisdom, restraint, and "tough love." It is not possible to describe one course of action that will fit every situation. However, it is possible to act with wise restraint and discipline, as opposed to an unqualified, blanket acceptance of such a person under the rubric of *love*.

Most churches have not considered in advance what they will do or how they will handle such a situation. Here are some general rules that a church ought to follow in some form. Note that every church is different and governed by differing rules, according to their own constitution and bylaws. These bylaws are overlaid with rules dictated by a denomination, so conflict could arise. If so, make sure you understand that your priorities here are (1) the safety of the members and (2) the protection of the church.

When a man whose "history" includes commission of a sexual crime enters your church, the pastoral leaders need to have a long, frank discussion with this individual. This is especially true if the criminal past involves acts against children. Some churches will take a harsh stand and simply not accept any man with such a past into membership. This book is not intended to suggest rules on whom to allow into membership. I am not advising that churches accept or deny membership to any particular class of individuals.

But before accepting a person with a past of sexual misconduct for membership, investigate to see what restorative measures have been made. Make certain that these steps measure up to a biblical standard that is applicable. Then you should include some minimum promises as conditions for being allowed into the communion.

First, the person should understand that there will be monitoring of conduct so long as he is in the church. The monitoring ought to be simple and nonaggressive. For example, if the person is at an outing where there are children, someone on staff should keep an eye on him. In a church social setting without children, there's no reason for such monitoring. If children are present but located in a particular room or facility, the children are monitored, not the restored offender. Monitoring of the man is needed if the children are permitted to roam free.

Realize that this sort of monitoring is for someone who has been convicted of an act against small children. If the past offense was against an older child or children, more intrusive monitoring will be needed. Use wisdom. Don't go overboard, but don't be naive, either.

Second, make it clear that certain actions will not be permitted, and even one infraction will be grounds for dismissal. Under no circumstance is he to be alone with children nor is he in any way to solicit their companionship, their favor, or to even entertain them in any way. This would include giving them candy or doing little tricks for them. If the crime involved older children, then include that group. Advise him that prudence suggests that he avoid activities where there are large numbers of youth, except the worship services.

Third, set out these stipulations and prohibitions in a written agreement that will be signed, dated, and witnessed. Make sure it is filed. That might sound extreme, but I can assure you that if there ever is an incident and the church is sued, the lawyer defending will be overjoyed to see such a signed document. It would be evidence of measures taken to protect the people. It's not just the pastor's word or a deacon's word, but a signed document. There is no "he said/she said" encounter in court, but testimony-bolstering competent evidence.

The range of things a church can do is pretty broad. Each church is going to have to decide for itself what remedial measures to take. Some will decide not to deal with the issue at all and simply forbid anyone so convicted from becoming a member. Some will take a position that they do not want to offend the brother. A few will feel it impolite to make such a demand on another. And, unfortunately, some will simply do nothing and hope for the best.

There needs to be a balance. The grace of God must be included in all of our reasoning. A friend recently came to talk to me about accepting the case of a man charged with molestation. I was reluctant. My feelings were pretty strong as I heard the story. I had no sympathy for the man, and the fact that he was going to spend time behind bars did not move me. But God impressed me to see him. I met a man who was genuinely repentant and who had come to salvation in Christ. God showed me that His grace is sufficient, even for men like that.

Even as I was hesitant to accept this individual as a client, churches may be hesitant to accept such a person as a member. Sometimes that is wise, as in a case where the validity of conversion or repentance is open to doubt. But also remember that Christ did indeed die to save sinners.

3

A Closer Look at Some Reasons for the Risk

FAQ What ages of children need protection against child molesters?

ANSWER *All children, from infants to teenagers, are at risk.*

An Age Group at Particular Risk

All ages of children are at risk, depending somewhat on the psycho-sexual makeup of the individual offender. However, one age group, boys and girls ages eight to twelve, seems to be more frequently targeted than others. In working with sexual predators and their victims, David Grimm has found that the typical child molester is drawn to children between the ages of eight and twelve years, children whose bodies have not matured. "The pedophile is looking for a relationship, a friendship with the child," Grimm said. "It's as if they were a child themselves. Emotionally, they are quite immature and they really like that interaction with children."[1]

Therefore, though all ages need protection, special attention needs to be focused on prepubescent children, because they are likely targets. Even infants can be victims, as can those in late teens, especially if they have developmental disabilities, or home problems that leave them starved for affection. *Assume that no child is invulnerable to a sexual predator.* Maintaining that mind-set will keep child ministry leaders wary. Statistically, most molesters are men in their forties, but sexual predators come in all shapes and sizes and ages. They can be children themselves.

FAQ   Why are most churches easy targets?

ANSWER   1.   *Little or no screening of workers*
2.   *The tendency to see only good in people*
3.   *Uncritical acceptance of a person's confessional faith*
4.   *Lots and lots of children*
5.   *Frequent unfettered access to children*
6.   *Lack of monitoring*
7.   *Untrained workers and staff*
8.   *The tendency to cover or minimize a crime*

Little or No Screening of Workers

Few churches have a valid screening process. Most ministries are volunteer operations, and when someone volunteers, the response is, "Praise God! Someone will do it!"

Some churches go through the motions of screening workers, but often the person doing the screening is a friend of the person being screened. Generally, leaders focus on whether the volunteer has enough strength and emotional stability to do the job; they aren't thinking about child molesters. The primary consideration is getting the job filled.

It's time to refocus. In addition to having prospective workers fill out an application, ask the following questions:

1.   Has an accusation of child molesting ever been made against you, whatever the circumstances?
2.   Has anyone ever expressed concern that you might have touched a child inappropriately or otherwise abused a child?
3.   Have any accusations been raised against your spouse?

Be alert if an applicant has had any past allegations, even unproven, especially if it is a male. This is not to suggest that a past allegation in itself means that the person should be considered a child molester. But you should certainly give more weight to the possibility and act with heightened awareness.

Of course, this information is only valuable if the person answers the questions truthfully. Consequently, you should give serious consideration to paying for a background check (see appendix F: "Resources").[2] This investigation is well worth what it costs. Not only will it give you some assurance that you have a good staff worker, but it will decrease the church's liability if the unthinkable does happen. Leaders will be able to testify that a background check was made for the specific purpose of learning whether the individual might pose a threat to children. Though this is no guarantee that an incident will not occur, it is a reasonable step to ensure the safety of your children.

There is a tendency to think that larger churches need to screen workers more carefully than smaller churches, because the smaller churches are more likely to know the character and background of a particular member. In one sense, this is true, but it does not remove the need for all churches to do screening. Any church, large or small, should put into place a policy of screening all its workers. Some insurance companies will demand it, even if the worker has been in place for many years.

Dan Burrell, pastor of Northside Baptist Church in Charlotte, North Carolina, heads a large and diverse ministry, which includes a school (preschool through high school). Pastor Burrell said,

> Today's pastor is being called upon to navigate ministries through a minefield of spiritual, legal, administrative, organizational, ethical, and regulatory issues which they are ill-prepared by most seminaries and universities to address. A wise pastor must seek outside guidance and accountability if he's to protect the reputation, mission, and safety of the local body of believers internally and externally. No single area of ministry is more vulnerable to litigation and tragedy than volunteer screening.[3]

The Tendency to See Only Good in People

The tendency in some churches to see only good in people can be detrimental. For example, the attitude that "we're only human" can cause leaders to overlook and excuse questionable behavior and serious moral failures. Churches can even be lulled into trying to excuse destructive criminality. A "woman with a past" is viewed as a Rahab, a friend who has come in out of the night and now is one of us. The church may glory in a man with a shady past and a colorful testimony, because he's "such a trophy for Christ."

The Rahabs are indeed among us, and we can thank God for the grace that brought them into the church. But we must not forget that their past problems could recur. The fact that each of us has some area of vulnerability and weakness to temptation should make us all wary.

Trust is not a bad thing, especially among people building community with one another. In fact, trust is a necessary ingredient for solid relationships. But having trust does not mean we do not protect those we love. The man who drives the bus that picks up my child for a church outing is a sinner just like I am. I don't know the status of his relationship with Christ. I do know that my trust of him is limited while my child's welfare is dependent on his actions. Therefore, I will be judicious in extending trust to him. I will not be suspicious, but neither will I be blind to the potential for a problem to occur.

In a church setting, every adult holds parental responsibility for every child. So we all should adopt the attitude of limited trust toward the bus driver when our children are on the bus. The feeling is not one of mistrust, nor is it one of suspicion. It is an attitude that acknowledges the depravity of mankind, acknowledges that we are all fleshly, and acknowledges that the potential for evil lurks within the breast of every human being.

Uncritical Acceptance of a Person's Confessional Faith

When someone comes to the pastors or leaders of an evangelical church, wishing to become a member, the individual usually makes a confession of personal faith in Jesus Christ. Churches have different procedures, but those that retain fidelity to historic Christian teachings have some sort of process by which individuals can be judged to truly have an internal Christian faith commitment and worldview.

Unless membership is granted only after a long period of association, church leaders are not in a good position to accurately judge the seriousness with which a person makes a confession of faith. Even with someone who has a long-standing relationship with the congregation, it is possible to "talk the talk" and even "walk the walk" outwardly without a saving relationship to Christ.

"Who knows what evil lurks in the hearts of men?" intoned the narrator of the old radio program *The Shadow*. We can't know anyone else's heart, and we barely know our own. What we do know of ourselves is frightening enough. The prophet Jeremiah said: "The heart is deceitful above all things, and desperately wicked; who can know it?" (Jer. 17:9 NKJV). Too often, the church has figured it out only after great harm has been done.

There is no way we humans can tell the validity of a profession of faith. When you came to Christ and joined the church, especially if you joined from another church, about all you did was make a verbal profession of what you believed. Another church might have sent a letter verifying your good standing and prior confession of faith. Beyond that, there was nothing. There is no trial period, and the body of believers accepts your word that you confess the same things they do. In time, you take on responsibilities, including leadership, demonstrating the validity of your faith with good works. You showed your profession to be valid.

If we are honest we admit to more suspicion about the confession of faith given by a professing Christian with a history of child molesting. While we may accept such a man into the church, my suggestion is that there should be a probationary period. Some churches may not do this without violating their denominational standards. Perhaps it's time to rethink such a restriction. Surely it is not too much to ask such a person to prove himself or herself, to show the validity of the profession by a demonstration of obedience over time. The apostle Paul brought a past with him when he sought fellowship and acceptance among the brethren at Jerusalem. They had reason not to trust him (Acts 9:26). It was only because he had spent time growing and doing good works, so others could observe him, that he was accepted. Others whose credibility was solid vouched for Paul. Reading between the lines of Acts, one suspects that, even then, it took time.

It should take time with a man who comes among you with a history of child molesting. Consider a one-year probationary period. But when that period is ended, don't forget that monitoring must continue.

Lots and Lots of Children

Just as a wolf follows the food, patiently stalking its prey, so it is with a sexual predator. He will seek out places where there are lots of children. He will install himself in the environment and structure. Then he will wait for his opportunity. He will be a chameleon, saying the right things; doing the right things; exhibiting the right behavior; modeling the accepted look of a Christian man.

Jesus told a parable about tares, a weed with a root system that intertwines with the roots of good grain stalks. Tares are a particularly nasty weed because they look like barley plants until late in the season. It would take the work of God and the angels, Jesus said, to finally sort out the good grain and get rid of the weeds (Matt. 13:28–30). False Christians also learn how to mix in with members of the church. We are not always capable of sorting out the good from the bad. If it were left up to our wisdom, we would rip up true believers by the roots and leave the "weeds" in the ground.

Because we know there are "weeds" in the field, we must keep our guard up at all times.

Lack of Monitoring

In scores of churches, it is not uncommon for a male worker to be alone in a Sunday school class with small children. In some churches, a couple may be in the class alone with the children for an extended period of time without a single visit from any staff member or other leader. The common reasoning is that monitoring is not necessary. Of course the couple is trustworthy. Unfortunately, that is the kind of mind-set that gets churches into trouble. Never set anyone above any particular sin, especially sexual immorality. And this is not about trust or the lack thereof. It is about being accountable to the entire body, to the parents of the children, and to God.

The danger isn't just that an adult might have access to children for a length of time. The danger comes when someone has un-supervised, unmonitored access. In most churches, monitoring of volunteer workers is almost unheard of. The suggestion that a program of monitoring should be implemented could raise eyebrows and provoke hostility. Such is the nature of organizations that function through volunteer labor. In a business environment, it is assumed that supervisors periodically check the progress and labor activities of workers. Sometimes, that is not the case in churches.

The attitude of most volunteer workers in the church is that they are demonstrating love and energy on behalf of the Lord and their Christian brothers and sisters. Monitoring seems to indicate a lack of trust, respect, and appreciation for their labors.

However, once they are acquainted with the bigger picture, these workers want to be responsible stewards and are more than willing to be accountable. It is an educational process. But unless the church makes the educational effort, allowing unmonitored access can open the door to a pedophile. The church actually enables sexual predation of its children.

Untrained Workers and Staff

Another problem troubles churches even when there is some effort at accountability and monitoring. Volunteers usually don't know the danger signs of sexual abuse. In one particularly notorious crime that was widely reported in the U.S. media, a young man admitted to molesting every child in a church nursery over an extended period.[4] Obviously, the congregation was not paying attention and noticing signs of sexual abuse trauma in its children. Any church that allows a young male to watch over the nursery or any other children's activity by himself is begging for trouble.

The Tendency to Cover or Minimize a Crime

Minimizing or covering for offenders is an extremely serious problem, and it can easily be criminal. Quietly reassigning or counseling pedophile priests contributed to the Roman Catholic Church's sexual abuse crisis. Certainly this is more of a danger in churches with a hierarchical or episcopal form of church government, but it is not simply a Roman Catholic problem. Non-episcopal church organizations have committed similar offenses, although they haven't gotten as much "bad press."

The instinctive desire of church members is to protect each other, or to assume that a report or complaint is overstating what happened, because the person in question could not possibly have done anything really bad. Protestants are just as prone to this as the Roman Catholics who found ways to justify their cover-ups. In retrospect, those actions seem to be horrendous decisions to hide the crimes of pedophiles, but they didn't seem so to the people who made them. Church leaders also become conscious of preserving the church's image. What if the ministry is pulled publicly into the scandal of a criminal prosecution? No one wants a scandal. Leaders can act out of a genuine concern for the weeping, remorseful church member whose sin lays bare before him. Perhaps they think, "There but for the grace of God, go I."

Such thinking has damaged thousands of lives in Roman Catholic parishes and left the reputation of priests in tatters. It also will end up costing the Roman Catholic Church billions of dollars in settlements, and more billions in lost donations from disaffected members.

Tale of a Cover-Up

A couple called me for an appointment. In my office, they told of the molestation of their seven-year-old daughter while she was in her Sunday school class. It happened in a very large and prominent Baptist church, and the molester was a deacon of that congregation.

During the course of the interview, it became apparent that the pastor had attempted some "damage control." In a meeting with the parents and the witness, a Sunday school teacher, the pastor undertook to defend the deacon against the charges. His tactic was a simple one, the essence of which was to raise doubt that any legal wrongdoing had taken place. He asked the witness whether the hands of the man were "under the skirt or on top." The witness replied that she had seen the man rub the child's genital area with his hand outside the skirt.

The pastor looked at the parents and said, "You don't have a case."

I recall that when the woman repeated the conversation, she looked at me with tears in her eyes and said, "We didn't come to him for money. We weren't thinking of a 'case.' We just wanted for something to be done. We wanted this man removed from the Sunday school class."

In the period after this initial meeting, the pastor proceeded to verbally shred the father, who was not a regular churchgoer and had a drinking problem. For several minutes, the pastor humiliated the man, seeking to induce guilt in him. It was a classic case of shifting the blame for the incident from the perpetrator to someone else. Later, another staff member did something similar in discussing publicly how "affectionate" the little girl was on his bus route. He told people that the little girl was "the most affectionate" little girl he'd ever known. He noted how she always wanted to hug him, with the implication that somehow the little girl's "affections" had somehow invited the molestation.

The pastor—from the pulpit—suggested that the accused molester should not be tried in a secular court, but should be tried, "if he's tried at all," in a church court. This, of course, showed that the pastor was placing the church above the law.

Lessons from a Cover-Up

In the end, that pastor's efforts to minimize and cover up the crime blew up in his face. It created a huge scandal and hurt the church and the pastor. To this day, many people in the community have a bad image of that church because of the way they handled the molestation accusations.

The case was later settled out of court, but the real damage to that church was not financial. There was irreparable loss to the church's reputation for integrity and witness for Christ in the community.

The lawyer for the victim, James R. Oates, told me, "I found it hard to believe that he [the pastor] could defend his deacon even after a jury found him guilty."

The community found it hard to believe, too.

4

Paying Attention to Detail

FAQ Is there a child molester profile? What should we look for?

ANSWER *Look for situations and behavior, not a profile.*

N o viable, working profile of a child molester will enable a pastor or leaders to determine who might be a predator. For example, age and marital status are irrelevant. Some "red flags," however, can raise the level of concern.

Pay Attention to Past Allegations

Be alert—to males in particular—when past allegations have been made, even if the charge was not proven. This is not to suggest that someone is automatically branded as a child molester after a frivolous charge or misunderstanding. But you should certainly take a closer look if accusations have been brought in the past. An allegation, though not proven, could still have been true. Realize that it is not always possible to prove cases. Sexually abused children often retract or recant what they have reported.[1] Matters might have been dropped for a variety of other reasons. Just because a man was found "not guilty" at a trial, or leaders in another church felt there was no substance to allegations, does not mean the man has done nothing wrong with children in the past. It merely means that the allegations or charges were not proven.

It is an unfortunate reality that a man accused of a sexual crime will always bear a burden. His reputation will suffer even if the charge had no basis and was shown to have no basis. But everyone also understands that the justice system is not perfect, and it is not always possible to convict the guilty. Especially in cases of child molestation, a case may not reach the courts. Because of the nature of this danger, even a man who has been proven truly innocent of the charges will likely bear the stigma, and raise fear in others, all his life.

Pay Attention to People Who Pay Too Much Attention

If a man in the church pays particularly close attention to children, be wary. Of course, this requires care and discernment. I love children. Many men love children in a wholesome and godly fashion. They'd die before they'd do harm to a child. What I'm suggesting here is to take note of men whose behavior just doesn't fit the norm, even ones who seem genuinely affectionate toward children but in an overly demonstrative way. Often, these men will demonstrate attention to children that completely excludes nearby adults. They will greet a child before they greet the accompanying adult. Adults are obviously of secondary interest. They will display affection toward a child in the presence of an adult, paying minimal attention to the adult and focused almost entirely on the child.

I'm not talking about a grandfather who hasn't seen his grandchildren all week. What should raise concern is a man for whom a focus on children that excludes adults is *usual.* And in this, even the grandfather is not beyond observation. Note where he touches the children and where he permits them to touch him. Is he slow to remove the child's hand from private places? Does he touch the child's bottom often? Such things are clues that there could be a problem.

Another clue is if a man spends an inordinate amount of time with a child or children *alone.* Red flags should fly if he *seeks* these times.

Always observe touching between adults and children. Look for inappropriate touching, even when it appears to be unintentional. Pay attention to frequency. How often does the man touch a girl "accidentally" in an inappropriate fashion? How frequently is the child's innocent touching of him in a sensitive place not stopped in a timely fashion?

When such clues are noted, put the man on your mental "monitor" list, but be careful about jumping to conclusions or making slanderous statements. You do not want to imply to anyone that an individual is "probably" or even "might possibly be" a child molester. Instead, you have to make sure that your monitoring of the individual is maintained vigilantly, especially if there are going to be activities involving him with children, at or away from the church.

Always Watch Someone with a Criminal History

Any male who has a criminal history of child abuse is automatically on the list of people to watch closely. If you're going to accept such a person into your congregation, you are taking on both a moral and a legal obligation. The law will insist that you had knowledge about the past of this man, and that should have alerted you to his propensities. Even if the man has a criminal history without a charge of molestation, it must be assumed that he has been in an environment of interaction with molesters—not to mention the possibility that he himself was sexually assaulted in prison—and thus should be carefully monitored.

Be open with the person about your concerns. Discuss it in a way that shows him that, as a Christian, he should be responsible and accountable and not give offense to any, or give rise to anyone's fears.

There also has to be more than mere observation of men with criminal records. They have to understand that their activities and ministries within the church are absolutely restricted. As a leader, you must meet with such a man and be direct with him. Do not mince words. Follow up that meeting with a letter in which you reiterate what you told him. Keep a copy of the letter in your files.

I believe that churches should follow a standard policy that no person who has a criminal record—regardless of the charge—can work with children. There are other ministries in which they can take part. If they have a record of sexual molestation in their past, whether proven or not, the rule is simple: No children's ministry. Period. It's not open for discussion.

While one might argue this is pretty stern and raises the issue of allegations made but not proven, the primary issues for the church must remain the welfare of the children and the liability exposure to the church. In a case in which I was consulted some years ago, a pastor called and inquired as to what to do about an allegation that was made against one of his male workers. He said he did not believe the allegations were true, but the news media would soon be at the church and he was not sure what to do.

Among other things, I advised him that he absolutely must remove the man from the children's work and notify the media that this had been done. I told him that so long as the investigation was underway, the man should not be allowed to remain in the children's ministry. I also told him to inform the media and his church (who would naturally read about it in the paper) that the removal of the man had nothing to do with guilt or innocence.

The pastor was advised that removal was also for the man's own protection. All he'd need was for another allegation to arise and he would be convicted in the minds of most immediately. To leave him in children's ministry if the allegation turned out not to be frivolous would be absolute disaster for the church in terms of publicity. Nor would a jury be as sympathetic to the church.

Some will differ with me regarding unproven allegations, but I also believe that once an allegation has been raised, even if it is never proved, a man ought not be allowed to participate in a children's ministry directly. This harsh-sounding rule is for the man's own safety, if nothing else. Child molesting is on the rise. In a room full of children, it is not unusual for a child to be present who is being abused by someone. Any subsequent investigation regarding such a child could lead to that man, regardless of his innocence. The investigation alone could completely ruin his reputation since one allegation had previously been raised against him. A man or woman who's had an allegation raised is flirting with danger to remain in such a ministry.

There must also be stipulations for men who come into the church with a history either as a sexual offender or where serious allegations have been raised. They must be informed about where they can sit and where they can roam in the church, especially during the services.

When services are out and parents are picking up their children, there's often a flurry of small bodies in motion. For most adults, accidental contact with a small child is no big deal. But for a pedophile, the same contact can be an opportunity or even a "turn-on." It may sound harsh, but unless you understand and appreciate the threat that a sexual predator presents to your church and its members, you will likely choose a "kinder, gentler" approach and learn the hard way. You must exercise "tough love."

Realize that even teenagers can be abusers.

Never let a male work in the nursery. Otherwise, you are virtually inviting molestation. You cannot count on the presence of female workers in the nursery to assure you that no molestation could possibly occur. In a nursery, female workers will often be busy taking a child to the bathroom, handling a crying child, or a dozen other things that can distract them. To minimize your risk, consider having only female workers in the nursery. Indeed, I would suggest that any ministry or activity where a child is likely to need assistance in the bathroom should be limited to female workers only.

In a society where the vast majority of sexual molestations are done by males, the lawyer's perspective is a simple one: *no males in the nursery.* Even if a female is with the worker, that female cannot always watch the male, and if it's her husband, she isn't likely to watch very closely since she trusts him. It may be that he is absolutely trustworthy, but that is not the issue. If your church is serious about safeguarding the children in the nursery, then the answer is as has already been suggested, to wit, *leave the male out of the nursery.*

I realize some churches will resist this as a mandate. However, if the choice is to have males in the nursery, then at least have several female workers in the nursery, in addition to the male. Some churches will allow the males in the nursery but not allow them to change diapers. It's a decision each church must make for itself. The legal mind is almost always going to choose the optimal safety, which I realize may not always square with the practical needs of a church. So I can understand when a church wants to involve the men in the ministries of watching the smaller children, including nurseries. However, if your church chooses such a course, please keep an awareness in the minds of the workers as to the dangers posed and never forget that it only takes one sexual assault on a child to devastate the life of that child and perhaps close the doors of your church.

It almost goes without saying that some actions signal danger: A grown man who wants to spend time with children but not with adults. A man wants to sleep in the same room or bed with children or take them on trips on which he is the only adult. If such warnings don't make the alarms go off, you may one day get the hurt of your life.

FAQ   How should I treat a member who is under investigation or who has suddenly been charged with child molesting?

ANSWER *Unfortunately, you cannot adopt the "innocent until proven guilty" posture with respect to some things concerning this member. Depending on the evidence presented (which may be substantial), you may have to exclude the person from membership.*

Whatever the evidence is, whether slight or heavy, you absolutely must remove this person from any contact with children, for at least three reasons:

1.   You do not know whether he is guilty. If you leave a guilty man in a position in which children are available, you risk a

second incident, which could be devastating financially.

2. The media will treat you with respect if they see you being responsible.

3. You need to send a message to the other members of your church that their children are safe and that steps will be taken to isolate individuals from contact with children if there is any question.

Some might feel that taking such a step is showing that you believe in the guilt of the man. That is a false assumption and can be dangerous, and you should insure that you do not send that message by your actions or words. Your responsibility is to the membership of the church. You cannot afford to place the church's future and the safety of the children at risk by adopting a legal standard (innocent until proven guilty) that is only applicable to due process in the courts. A church is not a court and adopting such a standard is foolish. You do not know whether the individual is guilty or innocent, thus it is imperative that the church adopt a position that says, in essence: "We want the truth and we want the matter investigated and a just finding made. We want the lawful authorities to make that determination."

You must be neutral. If you take a position that the man is innocent, you run the risk of losing the respect of the community and you risk losing members who may feel you don't appreciate the danger posed by the individual. If you take the (public) position the individual is guilty, you risk exposing the church (and yourself) to a civil lawsuit of libel and slander.

A police officer who is accused of a crime is immediately removed from patrol duties and assigned to administrative work in which there is no law enforcement responsibility and no contact with the general public. Depending on departmental policy, the officer's revolver may be confiscated and his authority diminished until the charge is resolved. Such administrative policies recognize that the primary duty is to protect the citizens. That duty supersedes the officer's right to a presumption of innocence. The department may unanimously support the officer and assert a belief in his innocence.

But still he sits at a desk. Likewise, a church must remove an accused person from every possible place of risk to the congregation.

FAQ   What should I say to the media when they appear in my office or in my church wanting an interview?

ANSWER *Have a prepared statement. Avoid speaking off the cuff with any reporters.*

Your prepared statement should include the following elements, at a minimum:

1.   A statement that the church has removed the individual from serving in any capacity around children.
2.   A statement that the action by the church has nothing to do with the church's belief in the guilt or innocence of the accused.
3.   A statement that church leaders will not discuss the case or the facts.

Personally, I think it is foolish to assert a belief in the innocence of the accused. How can you know? Defending someone when you don't really know the facts is not logical. The mere fact that you know the accused or have known him for many years does not lead to a conclusion that he is incapable of doing such a thing.

But if you've known him very well and for an extended period of time and feel you must give a statement of support, do so, but add a statement to this effect: "We want the system to work. We want him to be found innocent if he is innocent, as we believe him to be. But if he's guilty, our prayer to God is that he be found guilty and that the weight of the legal system would fall on him in full force." Assert your commitment to the children, the church, and the truth. If you are not careful, you'll give the impression to those watching in the community that you feel your church is above the law.

If you go too far in your remarks to the press and do not read from a prepared statement, you can be led down a path from which there is no retreat. If, for example, you permit questioning and a reporter asks whether the church knew of past charges against the individual, your refusal to answer will make the church look bad; and if you admit you did not do a background check, the church will look bad. And later your attorney will ask you why you opened your mouth at all.

So make a prepared statement. Have your attorney prepare it if you cannot do it yourself or if you do not feel comfortable preparing it. But stick absolutely to the script. Read it. Do not ad lib. And once you've read your statement, do not answer even the most innocent-sounding question.

FAQ Are there situations in the church that provide more opportunity or occasion for molestation than others?

ANSWER *Definitely. There are a number of key places where molestations can take place more easily than others.*

The Nursery

The nursery is a prime opportunity for pedophiles. It is not unusual to have to undress a child or change a diaper. It is not unusual to take a child into a bathroom to change him or her or to assist the child in using the toilet.

Outings and Trips

Church outings are prime opportunities for pedophiles to gain access to children, whether it's a ballgame, the circus, a youth event, or the church picnic.

Mission Trips

Whether in country or out of country, these extended trips may last a week or longer. Having a pedophile in the group can be disastrous.

Sunday School or Educational Classes

Who would have thought that a seven-year-old girl could be molested while sitting in a Sunday school class? The molester, an older man who had worked in the class for many years, was sitting in the back of the room with her, with no other children around, with his arm draped around her shoulders and his hand in her lap.[2]

Sleepovers

If your church sponsors overnight events, you need to pay attention. Whose house? Who are the responsible adults? What do you know about the man of the house? In testimony during the sentencing phase of the trial of the Baptist deacon who had molested a child in a Sunday school class, it turned out that a niece (who was flown in from a distant state) had often spent the night with her cousin (the deacon's daughter). During the night, the deacon would molest her. As a leader in the church, you can't be too careful in this area.

Transporting Children Home After Church

The deacon who molested the girl in her Sunday school class also drove a bus. During the sentencing phase, a woman testified that when she was a child, the man would always drop everyone off first and then he'd pull over to the side of the road and molest her. Never allow a man to be alone on a bus with children. Always have another worker, preferably a female worker.

Counseling

Molestations in this setting usually occur when a youth worker or pastor molests a teenager in his group. Accountability and awareness is the key here. Safeguards must be established even for staff members. Assume everyone is capable of falling into sin, insist on accountability, and don't back off from it.

Unmonitored Workers

What people do to children when they're not watched can be rather shocking. A nation was shocked when it saw a videotape of Madelyne Gorman Toogood abusing her child in a South Bend, Indiana, department store parking lot.[3] There have been stories of nannies who abused children in their care and a host of other crimes committed against children while an individual was alone with the child. I have already said that my lawyer's perspective is to exclude all men from the nursery. I realize some churches will resist this as a mandate. However, if the choice is to have males in the nursery, then at least have several female workers in the nursery, besides the worker's spouse. The wife will not watch her husband as closely if she trusts him. Trustworthiness is not the issue.

For example, it may be that as a church, you have a bus driver who picks up some children to transport them to activities on a Wednesday night. There are churches all over this nation who see nothing wrong with that man being the sole adult, totally unmonitored, delivering children to and from church. Some churches assign a man to monitor the bathrooms. He's stationed there and is actually allowed to go into the bathroom and assist the children, unmonitored.

Bathrooms

It is not uncommon for a child to get up in the middle of a church service and leave to go to the bathroom. Too often, there is no parent accompanying the child. It would be wise to set someone in the foyer to watch for strangers who might have come into the church. The better course would be to announce from the pulpit that the church policy is to insist that a parent accompany the child. You simply do not know who might have come in off the street. It's not worth the risk.

Church Camps

Camps can be a legal minefield for churches and religious organizations. Make sure your volunteer staff is trained about what things to watch for, and make sure they know to report any possible misconduct immediately to a responsible camp manager as well as to the church. Every complaint reported should be investigated thoroughly.

5

Safeguards

FAQ What safeguards can we implement in the church to protect us from sexual predators?

ANSWER *Perhaps the most important action to take as a church, and as leaders, is to foster the right attitude among the congregation about this problem, and underscore the seriousness of it.*

You must view sexual predation as a very real threat to the children in your church, and to the continuing existence of the church itself. The first thing that must be done is to develop in your staff and in the church itself, through meetings and publications, an awareness of the problem. Everyone must acknowledge that the church is vulnerable. *It is only when everyone sees the problem— from the pastoral staff, elders, and deacons, to the members at large— that they can take steps to protect the church.* Weed out the attitude of complacency, which can be deadly. Do not assume that "everything will be all right" because no problems have yet arisen. If you have not been hit, don't assume that you can't or won't be hit.

It Is a War, and Your Church Is a War Zone

Realize that you are in a war. Satan wishes to destroy your church ministry. Do you think that he will not send an emissary to infiltrate your ranks, wearing a disguise so as to gain acceptance? If you think it is not possible or likely, your church is setting itself up for a fall.

Specific Steps of Protection

1. *Screening.* Carefully screen every prospective employee and volunteer worker. If they have a church history, send a letter to their former church and ask specific questions. If they don't, conduct an interview with them. Ask specific questions, such as this one: Have you ever been accused by anyone at any time in your life of inappropriately touching a child; of child abuse, molestation, or any kind of incident such as that? Make notes of your interview and save those notes. In today's legal climate, it would be wise for churches to save notes and records of interviews and applications for decades. Consider implementing a digital storage system whereby paper can be scanned into the computer and saved on a CD or some other computer medium for an indefinite period of time.[1]

2. *Applications.* In addition to your standard employee application, insist that every prospective employee or volunteer who will work with children fill out a Children's Worker Application (see appendix A for a sample form).

3. *Interviews.* Conduct a thorough interview. This should be done by the pastor, or an associate, and one other person. The value of having more than one person conduct the interview is for later testimony and the corroboration of testimony, if necessary. Take notes or even tape the interview. If you tape it, let the person know the interview is being taped. But, at least take notes. Affix the notes afterward to the application. As already suggested, save the notes or tapes. Laws in some states permit a molested child to sue many years after the molestation. You could find yourself in a lawsuit twenty years (or longer) after an incident.

4. *Inquiries to references.* Talk or write to people who know the applicant. Ask some specific questions (see appendix B: "Questions to Ask References").

5. *Inquiry to spouse.* Talk to the applicant's spouse, and do not mince your words. Be direct and up-front with your questions, and explain why you must ask these questions.

6. *Inquiries to former church.* Write to a former church or churches. Ask some specific questions (see appendix D: "Questions to Ask Former Church"). It is generally not unlawful to communicate a truthful statement about a former member. For example, if a member has ever been accused of an inappropriate action with a child, there is nothing illegal about communicating that truth to another pastor or church official. Be careful about drawing any conclusions if there was never a conviction or even a charge filed. You can convey the reasons why no charges were filed, but if you convey the idea that, in your opinion, the individual was "guilty as sin," you may have crossed a line and may expose yourself to a charge of slander or libel. But do not think that merely because someone told you something about someone it is automatically "hearsay" and unreliable.

7. *Don't play lawyer.* You're not before a court, and the laws of evidence do not apply to ecclesiastical decisions to communicate concerns to another minister or to another official. If you have concerns as to whether you can lawfully communicate a matter, ask an attorney who is familiar with church law.

8. *Discuss applications with leaders.* Gather leaders who typically would evaluate this matter. Discuss your findings and make a recommendation to place the applicant in the job.

9. *Make a report.* Write a report detailing the steps you have taken in evaluating applicants or volunteers. A concise, well-written report will likely be seen by a jury (if it ever becomes necessary) as a "reasonable effort" to place a responsible person in the position. The safety of the children in your church is more important than the legal safety of the church, but if the unthinkable happens, if someone is harmed despite your best efforts, at least you will be prepared to show a jury that the church took reasonable measures.[2]

10. *Understand the laws in your state.* Both paid staff and

volunteers need to know that they are responsible for report-ing abuse and even neglect of children, or in some instances, even if they suspect abuse or neglect is taking place in the life of a child.[3] It is important they also know what the defini-tions of "abuse" and "neglect" are in your state.[4] Staff should know what their state law says about their immunity from prosecution for the reporting of a suspected case of abuse.[5]

11. *Every pastor must know the law governing his role as a reporter of abuse.* A pastor or associate pastor needs to refer to his state laws in order to understand the rules regarding pastoral confidentiality (clergy-penitent privilege) and what require-ments lay upon clergy in his state for the reporting of abuse.[6]

Policies That Protect the Church

Triplets Are Better Than Twins

It is not uncommon for volunteer workers to work alone, but this circumstance should be avoided whenever possible. Some churches assign two workers in a class or other ministry situation, which is better than one but still not optimal. But if that is all you can do, at least try to make the assigned pair male and female (or two ladies). Also, try to assign at least one woman to any class in which children are being taught. Better yet, recruit three or more people for the class. The ideal mix would be two women and one man. The more eyes the better.

Educate the staff and the men and women in your church to watch for danger signs in classes and in all other church activities. Give special attention to training the women since they will be the ones who are most likely to be involved with the children. Consider hav-ing some special sessions for them with an emphasis on sensitizing them to being observant of any inappropriate behavior on the part of anyone, especially a male.

Establish a reporting system where incidents are reported imme-diately to the pastor or other appropriate leadership. You may be surprised at how so many of the women are way ahead of the men in recognizing signs of abuse. Some women have had to deal with such things in their own past in some capacity and are already wary. It will be comforting to them to know they have leaders who are not oblivious to the threat.

Select, Train, and Develop Monitors/Supervisors

Monitors and supervisors provide accountability. These do not have to be women. They can be men who are proven and trustworthy. Their sole responsibility during the church time is to monitor the classes, including the nursery. They patrol the church grounds. It typically will be a dull and boring routine, which for years may bear no visible fruit. But it may identify questionable situations or stop someone from being hurt. And if there ever is a lawsuit, a church defendant that has taken steps to monitor the church grounds and supervise workers will have far more credibility with a jury. Be willing to go the extra mile for your children. Give your staff and volunteers literature to read and videos to watch (see appendix F: "Resources"). There is a wide range of materials available for training the staff of a church. Keep records of your monitors, including the training they have had and the meetings they have attended. Consider having a log for each monitor, a general log, or a training log. However you do it, keep a record of who was patrolling on what day, where they patrolled, and what observations were made. Include remarks, such as "all seemed well."

A Pastoral, Public Message on Policies

At least once a year, or more often if necessary, give a message from the pulpit that covers the bases. Spell out what is appropriate behavior and what is not. Discuss the need to avoid inappropriate touching of the opposite sex, particularly of children. Discuss how to prevent children from touching adults inappropriately. Inform your congregation that the church leadership will maintain a zero-tolerance attitude toward inappropriate conduct.

Take a tough stand. Make it clear that any man who violates these rules with children will be dealt with sharply and inflexibly. Make sure this message is recorded.[7] Inform the congregation that they are the eyes of the body and if anyone sees any inappropriate conduct toward children, they are to immediately inform the pastor or a staff leader.

Over-Supervise Trips and Outings

If the church sponsors an event with children, make sure to have plenty of volunteers to accompany them on the trip, preferably more women than men. Give each volunteer a "Tip Sheet for Trips and Outings" (see appendix E for a sample).

Do Not Sponsor Sleepovers at Anyone's Home

Have sleepovers in the gym or the church. Again, over-supervise the event. Give tip sheets as indicated above. If the sleepover is going to be at an individual's home and it is a church-sponsored event, there must be two or more adult women who will accompany the children. Inform those adults that if they observe any inappropriate behavior, they are to immediately take the children out of the home and to the church and call the pastor or responsible staff person. A trusted deacon was charged with molesting two boys in a church sleepover. No man should ever allow himself to be in such a position and no church should allow it. The legal exposure is simply too great for all parties and the potential harm to a child is not worth the risk.[8]

These instructions should be written, dated, signed, and then filed. You are memorializing a spoken policy. In case of an incident that leads to a trial, the church's attorney will be able to turn what would otherwise appear to be a self-serving statement into a piece of evidence with some impact: a corroborative written document, contemporaneous with the event in question, which tends to confirm the testimony. In short, written instructions are no longer just your word. They are something a jury can take back to the jury room that will definitely have an impact on them. You will have established a "reasonable" precaution.

Remember that supervisors on a sleepover who fall asleep may scuttle your "reasonable" defense.

Avoid Assigning a Man and Woman Alone to a Preschool Class

In a typical Sunday school class of preschoolers, a husband and wife will team up to "babysit" the kids. Because the man should never take kids to the bathroom, his wife will usually have "bathroom duty," which could leave the man alone in the room for considerable periods with the rest of the kids. It is not a good idea for a man and woman (married or not) to be in this situation. A third person should be in the room.

Let's say a child is being molested at home, perhaps by a family member. If sexual abuse is suspected or confirmed and the perpetrator is not identified, a male Sunday school teacher may be at risk of becoming a suspect. Occasionally, cases arise in which the real molester tries to place blame on someone else to divert suspicion. Worse, children may have a genuine fear of the molester and feel threatened. When forced to name someone, they may name someone they actually like or know because they fear the actual molester. They may name their Sunday school teacher.

In a two-person situation, the Sunday school teacher would have to testify at trial that, yes, he was alone at times with the children. In other words, he had opportunity to molest the child. And if the child has said that the teacher touched him or her inappropriately, the teacher will forever rue the day he was alone in the room with the child.

Never Assign a Worker with a "History" to a Children's Ministry

To be safe, never assign to a children's ministry a man or woman who has ever been accused of any kind of abuse, regardless of the circumstances. If an incident were to occur, to have knowingly made such an assignment would look foolish and careless to a jury, and they might punish you for it.

Do Not Employ—Either on Staff or as a Volunteer—
Someone Just Out of Prison

Give any man or woman who has been released from prison for any offense some time before inserting him or her into a ministry. Churches often hire parolees as janitors, giving them access to keys and other things that are normally not available.

Beware. This may sound coldhearted, and some will decry it and say, "Where's the love of Christ?" But as we have already argued in discussing the role of church leaders, a good shepherd will not put the sheep at risk. This is not to say you cannot use ex-offenders at all in any sort of ministry. Of course you can. But too often the loving, forgiving nature of Christians makes them naive, and therefore vulnerable.

A man or woman coming out of prison may have needs, and your compassion may lead you to open your arms. The church may wish to embrace this person fully and without reservation. But in reality, you have to understand that the offender has been in a world that is alien to your world and learned some things that may still be ingrained. You simply cannot afford this kind of liability.

Create a Hostile Environment

Create an environment in the church that is decidedly hostile to sexual predators. Make it known that there are watchful eyes. Take an aggressive, no-nonsense stance. Do not be afraid to assert your position to the congregation and firmly establish the position of the church. Urge everyone to be aware of these issues. Bring in experts to address your congregation on the subjects of child abuse and sexual predation. Men in particular need to be educated to make them alert. They tend to be somewhat naive about such things and think that a big deal is being made about nothing. Women naturally tend to be more careful and insightful. By creating a hostile environment, you will discourage any sexual predators in the congregation. They will look for easier prey.

6

It Happened: What Is Our Liability?

FAQ What kind of legal exposure does my church have if a child in the church is molested?

ANSWER *The key question is, what kind of duty, if any, did the church have to protect the child? Numerous factors must be considered.*

It seems crass to focus on legal ramifications at a time when a molested victim and the victim's family are in trauma, and the molester has demonstrated that he is in a moral meltdown. Certainly, proper attention must be paid to the people involved. Lives are in ruins, and the pastoral staff and the congregation are likely feeling more grief than if their best friend had died. But at the same time, the church must address legal issues as well. This chapter assumes that the worst has already happened and legal action against the church is at least a possibility. Church leaders must look at the liability issues.

The Initial Issue of Duty

Following a molestation incident, churches are sued primarily because they failed either to supervise or monitor a worker, or to screen a worker before allowing that person to work with children. It is essentially a negligence theory that says, "but for" the negligence of the church, my child would not have been molested by this person. The initial issue before the court will be whether or not the church owed *a duty* to the child and the parent(s) to protect that child from being sexually assaulted. It is likely that the court will find there was a duty, which then raises the issue of whether the church breached that duty, or, in other words, was negligent (see discussion below). Even if a church were to raise a viable argument that the church wasn't a "safe harbor," the court will focus on whether the church could have and should have, under the circumstances, made it safer.[1] The mere fact your church is in a dangerous neighborhood may, in fact, make your duty even greater than ordinary. A legal presumption will arise that you know that fact and having that *scienter* (knowledge) gives rise to a duty greater than might otherwise exist.

Was It Foreseeable and Preventable?

The court will also look hard at the issues of (1) whether the incident was foreseeable and (2) whether it was preventable. This is a progression in the determination of whether there was negligence. In virtually every case, the lawyers who undertook to defend those cases had to confront those questions. What steps did that church and church school take to prevent what happened? What monitoring was in place? What safeguards were made part of the policy of the system? What measures were taken to insure that the things alleged would not take place?

The ultimate legal question is whether the assault could have been prevented by the church taking reasonable safety precautions. If the assault was preventable, were the safety measures necessary to prevent the assault reasonable? The courts usually take a fairly common sense approach to this question. The question of what is reasonable is going to involve a number of factual issues, one being a matter previously discussed dealing with whether the church is in a "high crime" area. There are many other factors that would be looked at by the court.

Was the assault foreseeable? Was it reasonable to assume such an incident might happen? The more remote the likelihood, the less legal exposure. It may be possible to successfully contend that the possibility of the assault was so remote that it was not something the church should have taken steps to prevent.

Keep in mind that the unlawful actions of your youth minister, your pastors, a church employee, or even a volunteer worker may be seen by a court to be actions for which the church is responsible. For example, in Lincoln, Nebraska, three lawsuits were filed against a school operated by a local Lutheran church.[2]

One of the lawsuits was filed in the U.S. District Court in Lincoln, Nebraska, by a Colorado man for claims of abuse by one of the school's retired teachers. The lawsuit sought $1 million. An attorney for one of the unnamed state court plaintiffs said his client has suffered from anorexia and post-traumatic stress disorder because of the abuse he allegedly suffered at the hands of the pastor/principal. Another of the lawsuits asked for general damages, $750,000 for medical costs and thirty years of lost wages. In the third lawsuit, the monetary claims sought were $3 million in damages.

A church must realize (as the Catholic Church is now realizing) that a pastor or staff member may bring legal liability to the church by his actions. Almost every claim filed against a church involving a sexual assault made by a church worker will contain an allegation that the church was negligent in the hiring of that worker. A number of legal doctrines may be applied in seeking to attach liability to the church. For example, a plaintiff may allege liability under a legal action called *respondeat superior* (also called "Vicarious Liability"), which is a kind of "strict liability." That means an employer (in this case, the church) will be held legally responsible for the conduct of an employee's actions. The application of *respondeat superior* is unlikely to be applied in the case of a volunteer worker, but there are a few cases out there where a court has applied that doctrine in the finding of liability of a church involving a volunteer worker who committed an intentional act. For example, a woman seduced by a pastor acting in a counseling capacity was deemed entitled to sue the counseling center under the legal theory of *respondeat superior.* The Alaska Supreme Court held that an employer could be found to be strictly liable for an employee's sexual misconduct where it did nothing to monitor or otherwise safeguard against such conduct by an employee.[3] However, many factors come into play and a myriad of threshold questions will need to be answered before the court will find strict liability.

Keep in mind that virtually every court will look at the efforts taken by the church to erect safeguards against sexual assaults committed by a church employee or worker, particularly those assaults on children. The court will examine the duty issue very carefully, as discussed. If certain legal standards are met, then the court may rule there is strict liability. At that point, usually the only remaining issue would be one of a measure of damages.

You need to immediately take steps to minimize your liability. While a church cannot stop a lawsuit from being filed against it any more than it can prevent every instance of sexual assault, the church can take steps to minimize the liability as well as the financial impact even if there is a verdict taken against the church. The most important step your church can take is to insure that there have been safeguards (as previously discussed) taken by the church.

Remorse for Neglect Won't Suffice

Once matters have reached the courtroom, it is too late to change history. The assault happened, and everyone is sorry that it was even possible. Now the court will decide whether the corporate body of the church and its leaders are culpable in the legal sense. Was the church negligent? If the court finds that the church should have taken certain precautions, or finds that they were negligent in hiring someone or accepting someone as a volunteer, or that they should have better monitored the child or children, then the church may be found liable. It may mean that damages must be paid to the victim, and possibly to the victim's family as well.

Some Lawyers See Churches as Deep-Pocketed Organizations

In light of the enormous wave of civil lawsuits against the Catholic Church, this kind of litigation has now come to the attention of the general legal community. Many of them now see the "deep pockets" of the church, and some lawyers see churches as the next "big tort" and are gearing up to take on the churches of America. They are looking for cases. They are looking for victims. Thus, you have to be diligent in this area. You have to take precautions. If you don't, you will end up on the wrong end of a lawsuit.

Your attorney fees alone can be enormous. Sexual abuse cases are often aggressively prosecuted, with the plaintiff's attorney adopting a "no holds barred" stance. Your attorney (unless an insurance company is providing your defense) will spend a lot of billable time defending your church. If you lose, then not only have you incurred attorney fees and costs, but you may well suffer a verdict that is catastrophic.

The Evangelical Lutheran Church in America's Northern Texas/Northern Louisiana Synod had that experience when a jury awarded $36.8 million for sexual abuse committed by Gerald P. Thomas, former pastor of Good Shepherd Lutheran Church in Marshall, Texas.[4] There were fourteen victims. Settlements prior to trial brought the total value up to nearly $69 million, though there was some confusion over the final tally as some of the settlements may have been used to offset the verdict. This case had all the elements necessary to win at trial: *a duty, a failure in that duty to protect, negligence (that appears to be "gross" negligence), liability that reached back to the employer, and a system in place that was woefully inadequate for the protection of a certain class of its membership.*

This is not to say that every plaintiff's attorney sees churches as "deep pocket" defendants. However, your church may be identified as the *proximate cause*—that is, the "legal cause"—of harm to the child. Consequently, the lawyer representing the child and the parents has a legal duty and ethical obligation to pursue the church on behalf of the client. Our society functions as a nation of laws. When a wrong is committed, we do not, as a rule, seek to do the same injury to the other person. Instead, a common remedy is a monetary award, made by a jury or judge to the plaintiff.

Your church may be liable for the acts of a sexual predator if a jury concludes that you had a duty to provide a safe environment for children that included reasonable supervision and monitoring or screening of workers, or other measures designed to protect those children.[5]

Losses May Not Be Just Monetary

If a church is found negligent, the exposure can be catastrophic economically, as well as to the reputation of the body of Christ, and in the spiritual devastation that often lies in the wake of such events.

The reputation of the church definitely will suffer. Some members probably will leave, not wanting to be associated with a church that carries a soiled reputation. They also may not want to be part of paying off a large financial judgment. Even among members who stay, income to the church may be lost.

During the course of litigation, the church becomes an open window. The plaintiff's attorneys will be looking for "dirt" that will compromise the "good reputation" defense they know the church is likely to offer. There will be multiple depositions. It is not unusual for the entire staff of a church to be deposed, as well as several members.

Sexual abuse cases carry with them a high level of sensationalism. News media will pay close attention to the case and your church will surely be featured in several reports or articles. During the "discovery" process, the attention will typically diminish, but after the verdict, win or lose, the church will be featured once more. This kind of publicity damages a church's reputation, even if it is shown that there was no basis to the charge or little the church could have reasonably done to avoid the incident. Even if the defendant is acquitted at trial, many observers will say, "Yeah, he got off, but he was guilty." That will be a common opinion, unfortunately.

The ministry of the church certainly will suffer as members are distracted by the legal proceedings. Pastoral staff will be burdened by the allegations and the threat posed by them. The senior pastor often will struggle to concentrate on his normal church responsibilities and may even suffer a stress overload. Pastors and staff will be second-guessing themselves as to how they might have done a better job of protecting the child or children, but they will be prevented from talking much about it because of litigation concerns. They may feel there was something they could have done personally, but if they voice that concern, it could get back to the plaintiff's lawyer, who will certainly use that statement to incriminate the church.

For other workers in the church, it becomes a time of turmoil. They fear being called to give a deposition. No one wants to testify at a deposition, or in court, and lie. At the same time, no one wants to admit under oath apparent negligence: "Uh, yes, we should have been monitoring that room, and, uh, no, I guess we didn't have anyone else in the room with him at all those times." However, that is exactly the scenario that faces some church members in the aftermath of a sexual assault or case of abuse. Many honest workers have had to make such admissions. And more will surely follow, simply because church leaders *still* do not think it can ever happen in their church. It never happened before, they reason, so it won't happen in the future.

I pray that church leaders will wake up and take the necessary steps to safeguard their churches before some child molester disabuses them of their naive thinking. How sad that the consequences of being foolish are so great.

7

Sexual Assaults by Leaders

FAQ   What are the consequences to a church if the sexual assault was done by a pastor or leader in the church?

ANSWER   *The consequences are absolutely staggering! Of all the possible situations, sexual molestation by a leader causes the most devastation, both financially and spiritually.*

As more has become known about sexual predation of children, one of the saddest discoveries has been the astounding number of sexual predators among pastors, teachers, and others in positions of trust and authority in the church. Such sins should not be even named among us (Eph. 5:3). However, improper and even illegal sexual behavior is rampant in churches and often involves leaders.

The Protestant World Is Not Immune

The Roman Catholic Church scandals have mostly involved priests. Lest this seem to be a problem related to celibate religious vocations, look at all the cases involving pastors and leaders who are evangelicals, Pentecostals, charismatics, Lutherans, Presbyterians, and Baptists. Pastors have preyed on the weakest, most vulnerable members in their congregations—*the children.* Cases reveal that elders, deacons, teachers, and coaches in churches and church-related schools also can be sexual predators.

- A twenty-year-old man in King County, Washington, sued Christian Faith Center, alleging that church staff failed years ago to protect him from a Sunday school teacher who sexually abused him, although leaders were aware that the teacher had molested before.[1] This illustrates how failure to deal with a molestation allegation properly can expose a church to liability years later.
- A Danville, Virginia, pastor admitted to deacons in his church that he had acted "inappropriately" with a child. The deacons were subsequently shocked to learn that he'd been charged with six felony counts involving sexual assault on a child.[2]
- Joe Combs, a pastor in Tennessee and former Bible teacher at a large Baptist college, received a fifty-year sentence for his rape and abuse of a girl that he and his wife had cared for. The abuse had gone on for years.[3]
- An Assemblies of God youth worker was arrested and charged with sodomy and taking pornographic pictures of minor girls.[4]
- In Austin, Texas, a former youth minister was convicted of nine counts of child sexual abuse.[5]
- A minister in Minnesota was sentenced to seven and one-half years for sexual abuse of a minor. Settlement terms of a lawsuit against his church were said to be "under $500,000." Police said they suspected the minister had abused as many as one hundred victims in his past.[6]
- The Iowa Supreme Court upheld the conviction of a Cedar Rapids minister found guilty of sexually assaulting a female church member.[7]
- In Oklahoma, a coach who was a former "teacher of the year," church deacon, and counselor, was convicted on twenty-five counts of sexual abuse and molestation.[8]
- Steve Lamberson pleaded no contest to two counts of molesting a fourteen-year-old girl and was sentenced to five years in prison. He was the pastor of a Baptist church in Oklahoma that also had a day school.[9]
- A Lutheran church in Duluth, Minnesota, was hit with a law-

suit stemming from a sexual assault on a young boy. In 1991, the plaintiff, John Doe [pseudonym] sued Pastor Daniel Reeb for sexual battery, clergy malpractice, and breach of fiduciary duty. He also sued the church, Redeemer Lutheran Church, the Minnesota North District of the Lutheran Church-Missouri Synod, and the Lutheran Church-Missouri Synod under a theory of *respondeat superior,* negligent hiring, retention, and/or supervision. He also sued Redeemer under a general negligence theory.[10]

- Seventy-eight-year-old Gallie Isaac Sr., a popular preacher in Kentucky, was convicted of molestation and sentenced to twenty-five years in prison.[11]
- David Brimmer, forty-two, a former youth minister in San Jose, California, was sentenced to twenty years and eight months for molestation after being found guilty of fourteen felony counts.[12]
- Cameron Huffman was charged with twenty-one counts of child molesting in the state of Indiana after he admitted during a counseling session to being a pedophile. When his church learned of the admission, they fired him and notified the police. Huffman is listed in the Indiana Sex Offender Registry. He was convicted November 4, 1993, and sentenced to twenty years.[13]
- In 1998, a United Pentecostal congregation in Eastland, Texas, went through litigation after a married youth pastor was accused of molesting girls during church-related trips he supervised. The youth pastor had been appointed to the position by his father, the pastor.[14] This is an example of how a church can get into deep legal difficulties by not paying attention to the duty of care.

Accountability at Every Level

It would be easy to fill pages with reports of church leaders who have been convicted of criminal sexual assault—or at least charged.

Obviously this is a serious problem among Christians. Sexual misconduct, some of it criminal, is epidemic.

In each case mentioned above, there are multiple victims: the child or children who were sexually abused; the loved ones of the victims; and everyone in the church congregations. The local church as an organization also suffers. It may lose money it cannot afford. It may have to sell its building to pay a judgment. Roman Catholic properties, even church buildings, have been sold in order to pay judgments. Dismayed and disenchanted members and other attenders leave. Some may never again enter a church.

Pastors and leaders should take steps to assure people attached to their congregations, schools, and parachurch organizations that they are serious about protecting people and especially children. The process begins when the pastor and other leaders realize that they themselves are not above suspicion. Every pastor ought to want to demonstrate to the congregation that he is willing to place his ministry "in the open."

Pastors Who Counsel Women Are at Risk

Counsel for women, if we look at it biblically, is to come from other women (Titus 2:3–5). Most senior pastors, and certainly most lay church leaders, are not trained counselors. Untrained counselors put themselves in harm's way when they assume that role. Leaders who do counsel, particularly if trained, must follow rigid guidelines. Once made, guidelines should be enforced without exception. Stick to rules and stay within the set boundaries. Make it known to church members that they must abide by these rules if they seek counseling. Then there will be no surprises on their part.

More sexual sin involving pastors has been committed in the context of counseling than in any other setting. Temptations can be intense when a man and a woman are alone with each other, discussing intimate details, hearing confessions, dealing with personal pain for a woman who is vulnerable and in need of emotional assistance. That is simply not a good place for any nonprofessional male counselor to be, whether a pastor or a nonpastoral leader.

The Pastor Should Not Be "Pastor Do-It-All"

Less frequently than in past generations but still too often, pastors take on the role of "Do-It-All Pastor." Particularly in small churches without multiple professionals on staff, the pastor becomes preacher, financial advisor, businessman, counselor, lawyer, and janitor. Most churches now realize that expecting one person to fill all these roles is unrealistic, but too many still want the pastor to be a counselor, and that is a role he should back away from for his own safety. Pastors should counsel from the pulpit or stick to counseling other men. Find women in the congregation, older women who are spiritually mature and who have demonstrated wisdom, to do the counseling of women in the church. Frankly, I believe it is often pride that prompts a pastor to believe he has to counsel everyone.

The Rules of Accountability

Organizations structured for maximum accountability have the most assurance that allegations will not be made, and if they are made they will be baseless and not believed. Sexual accountability, whether with adults or children, involves at least the following ten steps:

1. *Males never counsel a female alone.* A pastor who must counsel a woman would be wise to have his wife or another mature, responsible woman in the counseling sessions with him. At a minimum, the counseling should take place in a room that has a large window in the door, or an all-glass door. If the door has curtains or blinds, leave them open during all sessions with the opposite sex.

2. *Advertise your guidelines for counseling.* Make it known that you have guidelines and you will follow them absolutely. Spell them out so there are no questions. This approach is in keeping with the aggressive, vocal stand you ought to take against sexual predators who might come into the church.

3. *Never ride alone in a vehicle with a woman who is not your wife, daughter, or other close relative.* Just make it a rule and abide by it.

4. *Insist that every youth worker, whether paid or volunteer, abides by these rules.* No male youth worker should be alone with a female who is not a spouse or other close relative. Demand it. Many will not like it. Those who resist the rule or who call it "legalism," are either ignorant or potential problems. Get rid of your problems.

5. *Male adults do not stay in a tent with children* (other than their own children). On outings such as camping trips, the rule should be that no male adult or older teen will stay in a tent with the children. This protects everyone.

6. *Diminish privacy settings for counseling.* All counseling should be done in as open a setting as possible. The era when one could do things in absolute privacy is gone. It is unfortunate but true. Leaders cannot afford to put themselves in potentially compromising situations. They do so at their own risk.

7. *Assume that a sexual predator will target your church.* If you assume that you have within your church someone who may want to abuse a child, you are more likely to take precautions that you would otherwise not take. You do not need to view every worker with suspicion, but you should view every worker as being capable of sinning grievously. We'd all like to think that no person who calls himself a Christian would molest a child. But as Jeremiah 17:9 relates, "The heart is deceitful above all things, and desperately wicked; who can know it?" (NKJV).

8. *Set up training for male and female workers.* Make sure that everyone understands the rules. Insist that workers report any and all violations of the rules. Make it clear that you are also responsible to them for obeying the rules. This is not legalism. It is about being prudent and responsible. It is about being wise stewards. Women must be made aware that when they permit themselves to be alone with a man who is not their husband, they set up potential problems. All workers must be aware that they could be charged with inappropriately touching a child. If everyone conducts themselves ac-

cording to the rules, it makes it much more difficult for any charges of a sexual nature to be made or found to have substance. All staff members should be trained to be alert.

9. *Put guidelines and agreements in writing.* Staff members and all other workers should sign a pledge to honor the rules and to conduct themselves in a responsible and accountable fashion. Insist that everyone agrees to report any violations of those rules. *Sign the rules yourself!*

10. *Publish the rules to the congregation.* Make the rules known, and emphasize the importance of everyone obeying the rules. The same level of enforcement cannot be maintained across the entire congregation, but at least a standard will have been established. By publicly announcing the rules (at least once a year), leaders establish credibility with the congregation of their good intentions. People know that their leaders are transparent and open about trying to be models of Christian love and maturity.

Some people might be critical of the church or its leaders taking a stand on some of these issues. Some people who want absolute privacy in their counseling sessions may insist that you violate the rules for them. Don't do it. Some may have to go to other counselors if they refuse to abide by the guidelines. But as people become accustomed to the good reasons why everyone should be held to a high standard, there will be new confidence in the church as a safe place with prudent leaders.

Another reason for maintaining these rules is that they protect male staff members from false accusations. False claims of sexual impropriety have always been made against men in the church, but now false accusations of sexual abuse and molestation have also become a problem. Juveniles have a level of sexual understanding that once did not exist among kids their age. If they misunderstand an action and feel threatened, or if they are upset with an adult leader, it is not uncommon for them to accuse an adult falsely. Once the accusation is made, the church is forced to act on that accusation and assume that there is a possibility that it is true.

Church Officials Have a Duty to Implement Policy

Church consistories, sessions, and boards that implement the policies outlined above do the church and its pastoral staff a big favor. Pastors and leaders who resist adopting policies that make them accountable and provide a measure of protection to the church should be questioned in depth as to why they do not want accountability. Be suspicious of such men.

Men in leadership who are true servants of God will desire and insist on accountability and will want to cooperate in a program designed to protect them and the church from legal exposure. Men who display an attitude of disregard for such things show evidence of a spirit of pride to the degree of arrogance. I would be at least as wary of such men as I would be of someone who came to the church with a prior allegation of child molesting that had not been proved.

FAQ   So what are we supposed to do when a report comes to us—or knowledge or a strong suspicion comes to us— that one of our pastors or other leaders may be sexually involved with a church member or a minor?

ANSWER *Act in a responsible manner and conduct a preliminary investigation within the scope of your authority and responsibility. Contact an attorney to determine whether you have a legal duty to report your suspicions to secular authorities.*

Church Officials Have Legal Responsibilities

It is very taxing for any elder, deacon, board member, or trustee to be thrust into an allegation of child molestation or any other kind of moral failure. Nothing about these issues is easy. Frequently, there is no solution that does not entail severe repercussions for the church and its leaders.

But a report must be handled properly and in a timely manner. From the moment a report of illegal activity is received, every church leader has a legal obligation, especially if the accusation involves someone in the church's leadership. Once there is knowledge or even a strong awareness that something may be wrong, any attempt to cover up or delay the report of a possible crime exposes the leaders and the whole organization to criminal and civil legal liability.[15]

The Importance of Making a Record

Ordinarily, a board member, whether of a secular corporation or an official in a church setting, will not incur liability for a criminal act done by another official, where there was no consent, participation, or knowledge on the part of that board member. Criminal liability adheres directly to individuals who participate in or consent to a crime. Consent, however, might be construed from inaction. That is why it is important for a church official involved in a board meeting or other official meeting to make a written and oral protest if the board decides to do something that might be construed as wrong or even criminal. Such a written and oral protest should be raised if a report of sexual impropriety by a leader comes up and the board decides not to investigate or take appropriate action. Make sure it is known that you did not agree with the majority. Do not assume that the notes taken in the meeting will be transcribed or placed in the official record.

If an official is cited in a negative report and has enough clout or cunning, no record of your protest may make it into the record. Even if the policy of the church is to present to the congregation a vote by the deacons or church officials as a general, unified vote, insist that there be a record of your dissent in the written transcripts or minutes of that meeting. Write it up yourself, if necessary. Send a copy by certified mail to the chairman or other official responsible for the church records of these proceedings. Save a copy for your records.

You need not go on the record before the entire congregation, but your dissenting vote should be recorded in the official records of the church. If you cannot agree with a direction the board is taking that might expose you to legal liability on a personal level, resign. But first make a record of your dissent.

Church Officials Must Act in a Swift and Timely Fashion

If your church has a pastor who has become a serious liability; if he's a man who refuses accountability or about whom allegations have been raised, governing board members must act swiftly and decisively. Most denominations have standards and step-by-step policies of church discipline, but these may not be sufficient to satisfy legal standards.

It is not within the scope of this book to dictate church policy with respect to the removal of a church official. Each church has its own policy. The worst dangers are in congregations in which autocratic pastoral leadership has evolved. If the pastor rules with an iron hand, much as the kings of old, the congregation already is in a lot of trouble. Leaders are faced with a daunting and intimidating task if there are legal or moral reasons for removing the pastor. Unless the people of the congregation take a stand, it can be almost impossible.[16]

If you find yourself in such a dilemma as a board member or some other church official, the best recourse is to find an attorney who understands church law. Such an attorney can tell you what steps to take to protect yourself as an official, and to protect the church. Although there is usually a solution, unfortunately it is sometimes seen most clearly in hindsight.

If you have personal liability in a situation, you may need to consult with an attorney other than the one who usually advises the church. But speak first with the church's attorney, voice your concerns about potential personal liability, and discuss whether or not he or she believes you ought to have individual counsel to avoid a conflict of interest.

FAQ   Are the trustees, elders, or deacons personally liable for a sexual assault by the pastor or other leader in the church?

ANSWER   *Possibly. It is not usual, but it is possible that deacons or trustees could be named as defendants in a civil lawsuit where a pastor or leader has sexually assaulted someone.*

The Plaintiff's Attorney Is Looking for Every Potential Defendant

As noted, high-profile sexual molestation cases have made churches a highly visible defendant in legal circles. A civil attorney who is taking on a tort case for the plaintiff will closely examine which entities or people to name as defendants. This is such an important facet of an attorney's preparation in a case that to exclude potential defendants can constitute legal malpractice.

Thus, the attorney may name church officials as individual defendants if he or she concludes that the officials enabled the sexual assault in some fashion. Perhaps they were arguably derelict in duties to protect the victim. Maybe they did not establish appropriate safeguards. Perhaps they failed to act while having *scienter* (knowledge) of serious wrongdoing or the real possibility of wrongdoing. Perhaps they failed to act responsibly in keeping with their official duties. If the failure seems significant and related to the acts charged in the lawsuit, the lawyer may name those officials as defendants. In the United States, some states have laws to protect against such suits, but many do not.

Leaders should beware of situations in which they become the "repository of knowledge," whether written or oral, which could place them in a legal "trick bag." For example, if you as an elder are handed information suggesting that a particular individual in the church has been observed doing something improper, or you are told that a person in the congregation "has a past" that would preclude him from contact with children, do not merely hand such information over to the pastor and expect that the matter will be dealt with in a responsible manner. Pastors are fallible people. The pastor may place the matter in a drawer and forget about it.

Suddenly, the worst happens. If you now say, "Well, I gave it to the pastor," but the pastor says he doesn't recall ever seeing the message or discussing the message with you, then you may find yourself named in the lawsuit as a part of a cover-up or part of a board or group of trustees who deliberately and intentionally ignored the harm being done to the plaintiff. While your legal exposure is not great and there's usually a measure of protection afforded to trustees and deacons, there is not an absolute bar to being named as a defendant. The safe practice is to make such things into a "big deal" and have a process or procedure in place that guarantees that information reaches all levels of responsible leadership within the church. The church discipline process may already cover such reports, or it may be necessary to design a confidential and appropriate process that alerts child care departments.

By all means, make sure the matter does not one day come back to haunt you because it disappeared into a pile on someone's desk or somehow was not acted upon in a proper and timely fashion.

8

A Duty to Report?

FAQ What if I am told, in confidence, of a molestation. What are my obligations?

ANSWER *Your legal obligations may differ from your moral obligations. Failure to divulge that information could be a crime in some states (such as Texas, for example).*

Every State Requires Mandatory Reporting with a Few Exemptions

In the United States, the first mandatory child abuse and neglect reporting laws were enacted by states in the early 1960s. Since then, states have been adding to their lists of the kinds of individuals and entities that must report known or suspected child maltreatment.[1] Since 1967, all states have enacted legislation requiring reporting of child abuse/neglect by many professionals, such as doctors and other health care workers, teachers, and school officials.[2] States differ in their reporting requirements. Some states attach criminal penalties to a failure to report.[3]

In many states, clergy—in particular, Roman Catholic clergy—have strongly resisted mandated reporting requirements. At this writing, legal challenges are still in the courts over some states' laws.[4] New Hampshire, North Carolina, Rhode Island, and West Virginia include clergy among mandated reporters of child abuse. Texas exempts no one from reporting child abuse. It isn't even covered under attorney-client privilege. You *must* report child abuse in Texas.

A Policy of "Zero Tolerance" for Reporting

To be safe, every pastor and church leader should consult with an attorney to discover reporting obligations for known or suspected child abuse. *Assume that there is a requirement.* If you're uncomfortable, meet with your church leaders and develop a policy of "zero tolerance." That means that *any information* about child abuse will be reported to the proper authorities. This includes anything observed or suspected by anyone with an official relationship to the church, including any information that comes out during counseling. Make it the church's policy to report all questionable matters to the proper authorities. Base that decision on scriptural foundations for life in the body, protecting the body from harm, and a thoughtful theology of the church's relationship with secular authority. While it is not the objective here to formulate biblical standards or policy, basing your policy on the Bible is not only mandatory for a congregation, its standards have legal ramifications. It can be important to a court that your position has a basis founded in the objective standards on which your group is founded. It demonstrates that the group is consistently teaching and following the doctrines they confess.

For example, it would be easy to use the following verse to establish a zero-tolerance policy: "And have no fellowship with the unfruitful works of darkness, but rather reprove them" (Eph. 5:11). Clearly, child abuse is one of those "works of darkness." It is difficult to reprove or expose something that must be kept secret.

This is a matter that must be developed within the church leadership in keeping with polity and doctrinal distinctives. The issue here is not to bind a church to my interpretation or exegesis of Scripture, but rather to suggest some ways to develop your policy around Scripture and make that *your* foundation. Some readings in 1 Corinthians 5; Romans 13; Titus 3; and 1 Peter 2 would relate in various ways to the issues at hand and ought to be reviewed when developing the policies. In your review of these sections of Scripture, consider the use of Baker's *Topical Analysis of the Bible*.[5] An excellent resource for church discipline is Jay E. Adams' *Handbook of Church Discipline* (see appendix F, "Resources").[6]

Ephesians 5:11, in context, is an example of a text on which one might use scriptural principles to develop a policy of mandating disclosure of such crimes. *Such a policy needs to be written down and approved officially.*

Make your position known to all. Once you have the policy developed, publish it. Deliver a sermon on it, and save a copy of that sermon. State publicly from the pulpit that there will be absolutely no confidentiality for confession of a crime made to any leader. State explicitly that if someone confesses a crime that he or she has committed, the staff person will be obligated to report that crime to authorities.[7] Thereafter, make sure that new members receive a written copy of the policy. You have now made a public record that you will report to the proper authorities any known or suspected cases of child abuse.

Realize that you also have set aside any potential excuse for using the clergy–penitent rule to shield you from telling authorities what you learned, or preventing you from testifying about the confession in a criminal trial.

The policy should be spelled out in writing and reviewed by anyone seeking counseling from a church staff member. Give each counselee a brief, written copy of the policy and perhaps even explain the policy orally. It is valuable to have prospective counselees sign the form, indicating they have read it. Although this is an extreme measure, it will avoid a situation where the counselor has to divulge something that was told in confidence.

Penalties for Failure to Report Child Abuse

Very serious civil and criminal penalties may be placed upon a pastoral leader who fails to report a sexual crime. This is particularly true when the pastor learns of abuse that is about to be committed or is ongoing, regardless of how the report comes to light. Of course, the consequences of abuse upon a child outweigh any thought of legal consequences related to reporting the abuse. On the other hand, I know of no substantive cases of repercussions upon a pastor who has divulged a confidence to save a child from a sexual assault.[8]

Statutes traditionally have a clergy–penitent law provision that prohibits use in court of a confession made to clergy by a "penitent." But the trend is toward removing privilege altogether. I know of no criminal penalties for violating confidentiality, but there could be ecclesiastical repercussions for coming forward with report of a crime. In the Roman Catholic Church, it is a "church sin" to divulge something said in confession. Presumably, the confessor might sue the priest. Not many juries would be inclined to sympathize with the plaintiff in such a case or be highly offended that a priest violated the confessional to save a child from being molested. There is no serious legal liability on a pastor who reports faithfully the words of someone who confessed to molesting a child.

Usually, "confidential confession" defenses arise in criminal cases. A defendant seeks to suppress a confession made to a priest or pastor. It usually comes up when the state has subpoenaed the minister to testify as to what the defendant said. Typical is a criminal case in Worcester, Massachusetts, in which a former Sunday school teacher attempted to have the confession he made to church leaders suppressed on the basis of the clergy-penitent rule. The judge rejected his motion, and the confession was admitted.[9] No doubt the court reasoned that confidentiality ceases to exist where there is a third party present. Under any circumstance, courts are reluctant to suppress confessions revealed by clergy.

There have been, and no doubt will continue to be, suppressions of confessions made to clergy. Certainly some clergy will continue to insist on the inviolability of the confessional. However, there is a growing reluctance to allow anyone to hide the crimes of others. If there is any legal justification, a court usually will admit the confession. And since the Roman Catholic scandals surfaced, there has been intense public demand that knowledge of child sexual abuse must be revealed, no matter what. Clergy are expected to come forward with any knowledge of child sexual abuse.

If the church publishes a stated policy that confessions of criminal activity will not be protected, anyone who comes for counseling will know up front that the pastor accepts no obligation to protect him or her from prosecution. The liability for revealing that confession to authorities is thus minimized. In states where there is a mandate to report, there is no liability at all for violating confidentiality. Some aberrant jury could always render a verdict based on a heightened belief in confidentiality, so counselors do need to be wary. Each pastoral counselor must decide in advance what course of action will be followed if such a revelation is made. It is good to know the individual state laws that would apply, as well as the potential penalties for not divulging knowledge of sexual or other illegal abuse of a minor.

Obviously, there may well be a choice between breaking confidence and allowing victimization to continue.

Most advocates for reforming the reporting laws insist that the following specific legal directions should be followed:

1. *Feedback to the reporter of abuse.* Child protective service agencies should be mandated to notify the reporter of the disposition of the report.

2. *Immunity for reporting.* Immunity from liability should be allowed to anyone who reports information in good faith. Immunity would encompass all other activities the reporter might have to undertake after making a report, such as involvement in the investigation, providing access to relevant treatment records, participating in case consultations with prosecutors and multidisciplinary teams, and testifying in court.

3. *Reimbursement of legal fees defending resultant lawsuit.* The person who made the report could seek reimbursement from the state for legal fees arising from the filing of a report, including defense expenses if a lawsuit is filed against the reporter.

4. *Remedy for adverse action taken against a reporter.* The creation of a special legal cause of action for reporters to sue anyone who takes adverse job-related action against them for exercising their legal obligation to report would be a deterrent to retaliatory actions against people who report instances of child abuse.[10]

9

Insurance Coverage

FAQ Will insurance cover us in the event of a sexual assault?

ANSWER *Probably not.*

Initial Defense Is Usually Covered

If an action is filed against a church on the basis of a sexual molestation, insurance may cover the initial defense, and perhaps will defend the entire case. Early in the proceedings, however, the insurer will file a motion for declaratory relief seeking to get out of the case. This is a declaration by the court that the company has no obligations under the policy. Most insurance policies have clauses that exempt the insurance companies from liability caused by criminal acts, particularly if the person charged is a member of a church's staff, either paid or unpaid. The insurance carrier may have some duty to defend if there has not been a criminal conviction. Insurance carriers usually do not know whether a claim is true or false. They may be bound to cover the defense of a claim, but may not be bound to pay a claim if, at trial, there is a finding that the insured is guilty or otherwise liable.

Every state has criminal statutes prohibiting sexual contact or sexual intercourse with minors under a prescribed age, and virtually every insurance policy will have a clause exempting coverage for "intentional acts." Sexual assault is an intentional act. It is important to know whether there is an "intentional acts" exclusion in your church's insurance policy, and you must understand its legal application. Consult with your attorney for clarification.

Coverage for Sexual Misconduct Is Rare

For pastors and leaders, some insurance companies now specifically exclude liability coverage for sexual misconduct, whether criminal or not. The malpractice insurance carriers for the American Psychological Association and the American Psychiatric Association insert exclusionary clauses in their liability policies covering those professionals.[1] In light of the volume of claims against ecclesiastical professionals, those clauses have found their way into the professional liability insurance contracts for clergy.

This is not to say that your insurance company will never defend on such claims. In fact, it may even pay on some claims. But the insurer's policy relating to such matters should be fully understood from the time insurance is purchased. And any assurances from the insurance company should be memorialized in writing. One insurance representative, Patrick Hirigoyen of The St. Paul Companies in Minnesota, noted that his company routinely excludes sexual abuse coverage for organizations where adults are dealing with children.[2] And where the company might be willing to adjust its policy for sublimits, they will examine the organization's stated policies and practices, which "show what values and principles they are following."[3]

It is not uncommon for a carrier to agree to an out-of-court settlement in which the accused party pays half—or some portion—and the insurance company pays the balance. Usually, this is because the carrier is locked in to defend a case that will entail substantial defense costs. Settlement then becomes a viable alternative that they are usually willing to explore.

Part of the problem for the insurance companies is that they are in the business of writing insurance for protection of professionals, yet it may also be seen as coverage for the benefit of a third party, i.e., the victim. Some courts are reluctant to remove claims against an insurance company early in an action, because the victim may then have no remedy.

But unless the contract of insurance is ambiguous, chances are pretty good that ultimately the insurance company will not be held responsible.

> **FAQ** If my insurance company says it will defend the case and will cover losses to the policy limit, do we need a private attorney?

> **ANSWER** *Yes! And be sure to get that attorney on board immediately. Do not wait.*

One attorney involved in a school molestation lawsuit and subsequent litigation with the insurance company said later, "Carefully check the exclusions in the policy and do not rely too strongly on assurances from the carrier."[4] He said this after the school corporation had lost on its claim against the insurance company to pay on the judgment.

Depending on the circumstances, it may be that you are covered, but don't count on it. The minute an act of molestation or sexual assault occurs, or if an unfounded charge is made for which there could be liability, hire competent legal counsel. Your attorney should put the insurance carrier on notice right away. Hire private counsel even if the insurance company indicates it will represent the church and defend against the charges. *It is essential that the church have its own independent legal counsel.*

Insurers Have an Inherent Conflict of Interest

Insurance companies have an inherent conflict of interest. If they see an out, they are going to take it. But even if they can't get out of defending the covered entity, they may not want to pay on a claim. If a reasonable offer comes in, you need to know about that offer.

Your view of "reasonable" may differ from theirs. It could be in your best interest to settle within the limits of the policy. Your insurance company may not want to do this.

If you have independent counsel who has put the insurance carrier on notice that he or she wants a copy of all documents and offers made, then that attorney can protect you in a number of ways. First, he or she can make an informed determination of the church's legal exposure to liability. If your attorney believes that there is exposure, he or she can look closely at any settlement offers. If an offer comes in that is within the insurance policy limits, your attorney can inform the insurance company (in writing) that you believe it is in your best interests to settle the claim—and he or she can explain why it is in your best interest to settle. What if the insurance company fails to settle and moves ahead and a jury verdict comes in that exceeds the coverage? Based on your attorney's earlier communication with the insurer, you may have a claim against the insurance company for the excess verdict amount.

All of this depends, of course, on a determination that the claim is covered under the policy.

Even if there is no coverage but there is a defense, you still need a private attorney involved in relations with the insurer. It is not uncommon for insurance companies to hire their own outside counsel; that is, a law firm employed to handle this particular case. This is not "in-house" counsel. These law firms make their living by billing by the hour. Assume for a moment that you are working for a large law firm with high overhead costs. A large insurance company is paying large dollars. Unfortunately for you, an early offer to settle comes in from the plaintiff. If you accept the offer, the need for your services will end. What is the level of incentive for settlement?

In making this observation, I can hear howls of "Unfair!" coming from insurance defense law firms. I am not suggesting that all law firms that represent insurance companies avoid settlements because they want to increase their billable hours of work for the client. But just in case, the defendant should employ private counsel to remove all temptation for a law firm to take that road.

Coverage or Not?

Before an issue arises, every church should have a lawyer review their insurance policy. Sit down with the insurance agent and go over the policy, raising questions and scenarios to define precisely the limits of coverage. Follow up that meeting with a letter memorializing the meeting. If you have been led to believe you are covered in the instances you've raised, you want a written record sent to the insurance carrier's agent that this is your understanding. Make sure you send a copy of the letter to your attorney. With a record that has been reviewed by all parties, it is no longer a "he said, she said" event. You have written evidence of what was understood in the conversation or meeting.

Within the insurance review, search out any provision about what is covered regarding sexual assault. Some insurance companies are willing to cover that risk. They are more likely to do so if the church implements policies such as those discussed in these pages. It is worthwhile to get quotes from insurance companies that have wide experience in dealing with churches. With such carriers, explore the various options.[5] For example, is it possible to obtain insurance coverage for the pastor? Some insurers offer "directors and officers" coverage, liability coverage on officials who have operational responsibilities.

Memorialize Your Conversations

This letter should go out on the church's letterhead. Typically, the attorney will ask that you draft the letter first, then he or she will review and redraft it. After reviewing your policy with an attorney and the insurance agent, send the insurance agent a letter, prepared by your attorney, in which your understanding of the conversation is memorialized, along with any representations made by the agent. The purpose of this letter is to make a record of your meeting. If later there is any dispute, you have a written record rather than merely your own recollections of a conversation that may have taken place years earlier.

Conclusion

A leader in a church cannot afford to ignore the counsel given in these pages. If you are in a church where the leadership insists on breaking the rules or refuses to follow some of the advice given in here, then you have a choice: *stay and suffer the consequences, or stand up and insist on accountability.* It's hard to believe that any leader would be so arrogant as to expose his church and members to harm, but history shows there have been such leaders and will be more to follow.

Please don't be one of those.

I trust you will pay heed to the counsel given here.

Appendix A

Children's Worker Application

Name:_____

Date of Birth:_____ Male:_____ Female:_____

Marital Status:_____ Children:_____

List names and addresses of three friends who have known you for at least ten years that we may contact about you:

_____

_____

_____

Please answer the following questions completely and honestly.
1. What experience do you have working with children?
2. Please list all churches that you have attended in the past twenty years. Include the address and the name of the senior pastor for each one.
3. Please list all children's ministries in which you have worked or participated.
4. List all of your addresses for the past twenty years.

5. Have you ever been accused of inappropriately touching a member of the opposite sex?

6. Have you ever been accused of inappropriately touching a member of the same sex?

7. Have you ever been accused of inappropriately touching a child or an infant or a minor?

8. Have you ever been charged with but not convicted of any crime?

9. Have you ever been charged with and convicted of any crime?

10. Have you ever been charged with any kind of sexual assault crime?

11. Have you ever been charged with any kind of sexual assault against a child, or had a charge against you that was stated as a sexual assault against a minor, or stated as a "child molestation"?

12. Have you ever been asked to leave a church or a ministry for any reason?

* * *

You may adapt this form by adding to it or altering it to suit your particular needs but realize that the reason some questions are asked in different forms is because some people will assign different meanings to different words so they can later say, with a straight face, that they answered the question truthfully.

Appendix B

Questions to Ask References

Please answer the following questions about [name of applicant], who has consented to the sending of this questionnaire (see attached).

1. How long have you known this person?
2. In what capacity have you known him/her?
3. [Name of applicant] has applied for a job working with children in our church. In your opinion:
   - ☐ He/she would make a fine worker.
   - ☐ He/she would do better in a different ministry.
   - ☐ I do not wish to render an opinion on the matter.
4. Can you tell us what other churches you have attended with [name of applicant], if any?
5. Are you aware of any allegations made or charges or complaints ever made against this person of an improper or inappropriate touching of another person, including a child or children, even if they were deemed to be unfounded or untrue?
6. To your knowledge, has [name of applicant] ever been asked to leave a church? If so, do you know why and from what church or churches?

Date: _____ Signature: _____

* * *

Note that referral questions sent to a friend usually will not produce a negative response. But they might! Moreover, realize that part of the reason for questioning references is to show that you have made an attempt to examine the background and suitability of this person to work with children from people who know him or her best. In the event of litigation, this form could ultimately end up before a jury, and it would work in your favor. Also, when volunteers fill out the application, show them the form that will be sent to the references. If an applicant refuses to consent to sending the form to his or her friends, then you should avoid having that person work with children. Assign him or her to some other area of the ministry but not with children.

Appendix C

Consent by Volunteer Worker

The undersigned, [name of individual applicant], hereby authorizes the communication by [name of your church] to such individuals and/or churches as I have listed on my application for the purpose of making inquiry into my fitness to work in the children's ministries of this church. I understand that I do not have, and will not have, the right to read or review what was said by those persons, and I agree that their response will be a confidential document that is open for review only by a person or persons on the paid staff of this church and no others, excepting in a court of proper jurisdiction should said document ever become relevant in any proceedings.

Date: _____ **Signature:** _____

Printed Name: _____

* * *

The importance of this document is fourfold:
1. It provides notice to the applicant that this is serious business, and you will, in fact, be reviewing his or her past.
2. It provides you with legal protection for the communication so there is less chance of an issue arising as a result of a contact to another church or a friend listed as a reference.

3. It gives the applicant the very clear understanding that you are looking down the road to any possible legal actions where the chuch and friend's response might be relevant.
4. It gives the church and the friend notice that their response could end up being reviewed in a court of law, thus giving them greater motivation to be honest in their opinion.

You may lose volunteer workers as a result of these forms; that is, they may see the forms and decide they do not wish to continue with the application. That is great news for you! If they do not want to be open about their church history and their past, then that's all right. You have eliminated a potential legal liability to the church, and, more important, you may have eliminated a threat to the children in the church.

Appendix D

Questions to Ask Former Church

[Name of applicant] has applied for [title and description of position] in our church. It involves working with children. Our policy is to carefully screen those who work with children. [Name of applicant] has signed a consent (enclosed) to make inquiry to you for the release of information regarding his/her time in your church.

1. When was [name of applicant] a member of your church?
2. Was [name of applicant] ever disciplined for any matter in your church? If so, please indicate the reason.
3. Has [name of applicant] ever been accused, or have allegations against [name of applicant] ever been made, whether formal or informal, whether written or unwritten, of any of the following matters:
   • Inappropriate touching of any female or male.
   • Sexual misconduct with any adult or child.
   • Arrests for possession or distribution of any pornographic material.
4. Has [name of applicant] ever had any problems, to your knowledge, with pornography?
5. [Name of applicant] has applied for a job working with children in our church. In your opinion:
   ☐ He/she would make a fine worker.
   ☐ He/she would do better in a different ministry.
   ☐ I do not wish to render an opinion on the matter.

Date: _____ Signature:_____

Printed Name / Title of Church: _____

* * *

The importance of this document is that it demonstrates your efforts to screen workers before allowing them to work with children. You have attempted to assure that all applicants who work with the children in your church do not have prior allegations in their past. If you fail to get a response from the pastor of a prior church, send another form—only, this time, send it by certified mail. It will show you at least tried. If the certified letter is refused, when it returns put it in the applicant's file.

Appendix E

Tip Sheet
for Trips and Outings

Attention, adults! Please review the following guidelines carefully. It is important that you follow church policy, and that you implement the suggestions and tips given here during this outing so as to better protect the children in your care.

1. Count heads constantly. Be aware of where the children are at all times. It is easy to be distracted. Children have a tendency to wander.

2. As an adult chaperone, you are the one in charge, not the children. If at any time you feel you are losing control of the situation or cannot maintain safe control of the children, please contact the church immediately. The following names and phone numbers are given for contact in the event of any emergency of any kind: [list contact persons, *including the pastor's number,* and phone numbers; also list a local police number, local hospital/emergency number].

3. This is a church-sponsored event. This means that those who are in charge of the children are the ones responsible for their care. If another male who is not a father or sibling or legal guardian wishes to be alone with a child or children, you cannot permit them to take the child from your presence, nor can you leave them in charge of the children (except, of course, in an emergency). This includes grandfathers, uncles, or other relatives. This may be difficult to do, and if it becomes a problem, immediately make a call to the church or to the pastor or other responsible staff member.

4. Be alert for an attempt by *any male* to manipulate a situation so that he will be alone with a child in your care. If a male child needs

bathroom assistance, it is preferable that the female take the child into the ladies bathroom and assist, if the child is so young that he needs assistance. If that's a problem, then the male will need to do the assisting. But if so, the preferred rule is that another adult be with him, if possible. If a child goes into a public bathroom, the adult ought to enter the bathroom first to see if there are individuals in there and if so, then he needs to stand by the entryway while the child goes into the bathroom and check inside briefly from time to time. It's impossible to always have two individuals to go with a child into a bathroom, but adult entry into that bathroom should be minimal. Mainly adults should enter only to check for safety and to insure the child is unharmed. The rule here is one of prudence and care.

5. Strangers are often attracted to groups of children and may follow you. Be alert to these kinds of things. If you notice a male who is not a part of your group and seems to have an interest or seems to be following the group, do not hesitate to have an adult male from your group (or yourself) go up to the individual and make a polite inquiry as to the stranger's interest in your group. Only do this if other members of the public are around or if a male adult is present. If you feel anyone or anything poses a substantive threat, take the children out of danger immediately. Get to a public location, even if it means cutting short your planned event. The safety of the children is first priority.

6. If you are an adult woman riding on a bus or in a van as a worker, make sure you are not sitting in the front. Preferably, the adult male or men ought to sit in or near the front of the bus. If they sit at midpoint, they should sit alone or with another man. If you are an adult male, you should position yourself in such a way that you can observe the children without ever sitting in close contact with any child, male or female. The preferred policy is that an adult male never sit with a child or children, unless it is his own child or children. This is for the adult male's protection as much as for the protection of church and children. The adult woman should sit near the rear of the bus, thus enabling her to monitor the entire bus. This configuration of where the men and the women sit is particularly true for any long trips or night trips. Also, monitor

the children themselves to insure there is no child who is being abused by another child. It is, unfortunately, something that does happen.

7. Please insure that every male reads this. If you are in charge of this outing or event, then you have some serious responsibilities. One of those responsibilities is to insure that the policies of the church are followed, especially as it relates to not having any male adult alone with a child or children. This is for your own protection as well as that of the church. A false accusation raised against a man could be almost as devastating as a valid accusation. Where our policy is followed, an accusation can be quickly investigated and shown to be false because of our adherence to the rule of not permitting one male adult to be alone with a child. Realize that in that group of children there may in fact be a child who is being molested, perhaps at home, at school, or somewhere else. It could be that an allegation raised against a worker, although false, would seem to have merit because there was in fact a molestation. By adhering to the church policy, you can show the allegation is false, or at least highly improbable. For prudence, please comply strictly with our policies.

* * *

You may wish to have adults sign at the bottom to indicate they have read and accept the policy and will abide by it. The policy as written does have some drawbacks. If you get a careless worker who ignores the rules, the policy could certainly be used in court to show that you absolutely knew the dangers. But it's easy enough for a competent lawyer to prove that anyway, so I wouldn't worry too much about that. The focus in determining liability would then be on your "hiring" or use of that negligent worker. Indeed, it could be that you cannot escape liability for a negligent worker, and that his or her actions will be deemed to be the negligence of the church. This will depend on your church and the laws governing your state. Have your attorney review this policy and approve it or modify it as needed.

Appendix F

Resources

1. Churchstaffing.com: churchstaffing.com

This site provides access for churches doing background checks. There is a cost for the services but the cost of *not* doing a background might be much higher. Some of the listed costs are as follows:

- National Criminal File $25.00
- State Sexual Offender   9.00
- State Criminal Database (25 states)   5.00
- Federal Courthouse   16.00
- Credit File   9.00
- Motor Vehicle Check   5.00
- Social Security   3.00
- Identity Verification (Introscan)   9.75
- Education Verification   12.00
- Employment Verification   13.00

2. ChurchLawToday.com: churchlawtoday.com

This site is a subscriber-only site, but the fees are minimal. There are some restrictions as to who can access the site. For example, only local churches can access the "Basic Leadership Support Program" (at $1 a week), which gives "unlimited access for all clergy, paid staff members, treasurer, and church board members." If you are an agency of a denomination or a *parachurch* ministry, a law office, a CPA firm, a library or any other business or professional, you must select the "Full Leadership Support Program." At $1.50 a week, the cost is still a bargain.

This is a site rich in resources that any church, large or small, would find helpful. It includes documents, seminars, and an interactive forum. Attorney Richard Hammer, one of the editors of *Church Law and Tax Report,* is one of the expert contributors to the materials and seminars and other offerings. *Church Law and Tax Report* offers some videos and some audio recordings that are excellent for training and educational purposes of larger audiences on protecting the church against child abuse.

3. Child Molestation Research and Prevention Institute: child molestationprevention.org/pages/resources.html

This site is rich in resources and can point you to a wide array of other sites dealing with child molestation and its prevention.

4. Public Record Finder.com: publicrecordfinder.com

Excellent resource for locating sex offender information in the various states.

5. Sexoffender.com: sexoffender.com

This is a very good site with some pretty substantial resources. Check it out!

6. Restoration Resources

For some excellent resources for the restoration process necessary if your church is going to accept into membership an individual with any kind of a sexual misconduct past see the following:

- Michael Smith, *Restoring the Fallen: Guidelines for Restoration* (Green Forest, Ark.: New Leaf, 1991).
- Earl Wilson et al., *Restoring the Fallen: A Team Approach to Caring, Confronting and Reconciling* (Downers Grove, Ill.: InterVarsity, 1997).
- Jay E. Adams, *Handbook of Church Discipline* (Grand Rapids: Zondervan, 1986).

Appendix G

Mandatory Reporters of Child Abuse and Neglect (United States)

Each state and U.S. territory designates individuals, typically by professional group, who are mandated by law to report child maltreatment. Any person, however, may report incidents of abuse or neglect.[1]

Individuals Typically Mandated to Report

Individuals typically designated as mandatory reporters have frequent contact with children. Such individuals include:

- health care workers
- school personnel
- child care providers
- social workers
- law enforcement officers
- mental health professionals

Some states also mandate animal control officers, veterinarians, commercial film or photograph processors, substance abuse counselors, and firefighters to report abuse or neglect. Four states—Alaska, Arkansas, Connecticut, and South Dakota—include domestic violence workers on the list of mandated reporters. Approximately eighteen states require all citizens to report suspected abuse or neglect regardless of profession.[2]

Standard for Making a Report

Typically a report must be made when the reporter suspects or has reasons to suspect that a child has been abused or neglected.

Privileged Communications

Approximately thirty-four states and territories specify in their reporting laws when a communication is privileged.

Privileged communications, which is the statutory recognition of the right to maintain the confidentiality of communications between professionals and their clients or patients, are exempt from mandatory reporting laws.[3] The privilege most widely recognized by the states is that of attorney-client communications.

The privilege pertaining to clergy-penitent also is frequently recognized but limited to situations in which a clergyperson becomes aware of child abuse through confession or in the capacity of spiritual advisor. However, five states—New Hampshire, North Carolina, Rhode Island, Texas, and West Virginia—deny the clergy-penitent privilege. Very few states recognize the physician-patient and mental health professional-patient privileges as exempt from mandatory reporting laws.

For a complete listing of individual state laws regarding mandatory reporters of child abuse and neglect, see the pdf-format document on the Department of Health and Human Services Web site at nccanch.acf. hhs.gov/general/legal/statutes/manda.pdf. While this information applies only to the United States, those under other national and territorial jurisdictions should check for the same kinds of provisions with legal counsel or through sources of legal information.

Appendix H

Penalties for Failure to Report (United States)

Many cases of child abuse or neglect are neither reported nor investigated even when suspected by professionals.[1] Therefore, almost every U.S. state and territory imposes penalties, in the form of a fine or imprisonment, on those who "knowingly" and/or "willfully" fail to report. Also, in order to prevent malicious or intentional reporting of cases that are not founded, several states and territories impose additional penalties for false reports of child abuse or neglect.

Penalties for Failure to Report

Approximately forty-six states, the District of Columbia, and the U.S. territories of American Samoa, Guam, Northern Mariana Islands, Puerto Rico, and the U.S. Virgin Islands have enacted statutes specifying the penalties for failure to report child abuse or neglect.[2] Of these jurisdictions, approximately thirty-three states, the District of Columbia, and the territories use a "knowingly," "knows or should have known," and/or "willfully" standard. Other standards include "intentionally" and "purposely." A few states impose penalties without providing a standard. Failure to report is classified as a misdemeanor in approximately thirty-five states and American Samoa, Puerto Rico, and the Virgin Islands, while in Arizona, Illinois, and Guam, subsequent violations are classified as felonies.

Penalties for False Reports

Approximately thirty-one states and Puerto Rico and the Virgin Islands have statutes specifying penalties for false reports of child abuse or neglect. The most common standards are "knowingly" and/or "willfully." The penalties imposed are similar to those for failure to report. The majority of states classify false reporting as a misdemeanor. In nine states, a false report may be classified as a felony under specific circumstances.

To see a complete listing of U.S. state laws regarding mandatory reporters of child abuse and neglect, see the pdf-format document on the Department of Health and Human Services Web site at nccanch.acf.hhs.gov/general/legal/statutes/report.pdf. While this information applies only to the United States, those under other national and territorial jurisdictions should check for the same kinds of provisions with legal counsel or through sources of legal information.

Appendix I

Definitions of Child Abuse and Neglect

It can be important to understand some definitions of child abuse as applied in the government jurisdiction under which you live and work.[1] There may be a requirement to report any type of abuse that you see or suspect. There are various definitions, and it would be worth your while to peruse the law. If you have any questions about what constitutes child abuse, call your attorney and request he or she explain the meaning as it relates to your particular state.

In the United States, child abuse and neglect are defined by both federal and state legislation. The Child Abuse Prevention and Treatment Act (CAPTA) is the federal legislation that provides minimum guidelines that states must incorporate in their statutory definitions of child abuse and neglect.

Based on CAPTA guidelines, each state and U.S. territory provides its own definitions of child abuse and neglect. As applied to reporting statutes, these definitions describe the acts and conditions that determine the grounds for state intervention in the protection of a child's well-being.

Standards

The standard for what constitutes abuse varies among states. Many states define abuse in terms of "harm or threatened harm" to a child's health or welfare. A few states define abuse in terms of "serious harm or threat of serious harm."

Most statutes also specify exceptions. The most common exception is a religious exemption for parents who choose not to seek medical care for their children due to religious beliefs. Other exceptions include corporal punishment, cultural practices, and poverty.

Categories

States generally provide separate definitions for physical abuse, neglect, sexual abuse, sexual exploitation, and emotional maltreatment. Many states and territories now include abandonment in their definition of neglect. Some definitions are detailed, while others are broad. States with broader definitions provide Child Protective Services (CPS) with greater discretion in determining what constitutes abuse.

To see how individual states address this issue, see the pdf-format document on the Department of Health and Human Services Web site nccanch .acf.hhs.gov/general/legal/statutes/define.pdf.

Appendix J

Clergy as Mandatory Reporters of Child Abuse and Neglect

A mandatory reporter is a person who is required to report suspected cases of child abuse and neglect.[1] Every state, the District of Columbia, and the U.S. territories have statutes that identify mandatory reporters of child maltreatment and specify the circumstances under which they are to report.

Approximately twenty-five states—Alabama, Arizona, Arkansas, California, Colorado, Connecticut, Illinois, Louisiana, Maine, Massachusetts, Michigan, Minnesota, Mississippi, Missouri, Montana, Nevada, New Hampshire, New Mexico, North Dakota, Oregon, Pennsylvania, South Carolina, Vermont, West Virginia, and Wisconsin—currently include members of the clergy among those professionals specifically mandated by those states' reporting laws to report known or suspected instances of child abuse or neglect. In approximately eighteen states—Delaware, Florida, Idaho, Indiana, Kentucky, Maryland, Mississippi, Nebraska, New Hampshire, New Jersey, New Mexico, North Carolina, Oklahoma, Rhode Island, Tennessee, Texas, Utah, and Wyoming—and Puerto Rico, any person who suspects child abuse or neglect is required to report. That broad language appears on its face to include clergy as well as anyone else, but it is possible that the term has been interpreted otherwise.

Privileged Communications

As a doctrine of some theological traditions, clergy must maintain the confidentiality of pastoral communications. Mandatory reporting statutes in some states specify when a communication is privileged. "Privileged communications" is the statutory recognition of the right to maintain the confidentiality of such communications. Privileged communications may be exempt from the reporting laws. The privilege of maintaining this confidentiality under state law must be provided by statute, and most states do provide the privilege, typically in rules of evidence or civil procedure.

If the issue of privilege is not addressed in the reporting laws, it does not mean that privilege is not granted; it may be granted in other parts of state statutes.

This privilege, however, is not absolute. While clergy-penitent privilege is frequently recognized within the reporting laws, it is typically interpreted narrowly in the child abuse or neglect context. The circumstances under which it is allowed vary from state to state, and in some states it is denied altogether. For example, among the states that enumerate clergy as mandated reporters, New Hampshire and West Virginia deny the clergy-penitent privilege in cases of child abuse or neglect. Three states that enumerate "any person" as a mandated reporter—North Carolina, Rhode Island, and Texas—also deny clergy-penitent privilege in child abuse cases.

In states where neither clergy nor "any person" are enumerated as mandated reporters, it is less clear whether clergy are included as mandated reporters within other broad categories of professionals who work with children. For example, in Washington clergy are not enumerated as mandated reporters, but the clergy-penitent privilege is affirmed within the reporting laws.

Many states and territories include Christian Science practitioners or religious healers among professionals who are mandated to report suspected child maltreatment. In most instances, they appear to be regarded as a type of health care provider. Only eight states—Arizona, Arkansas, Louisiana, Massachusetts, Missouri, Nevada, South Carolina, and Vermont—explicitly include Christian Science practitioners among classes of clergy required to report. The clergy-penitent privilege is also extended to those practitioners by statute.

Clergy as Mandated Reporter (United States)

States in which clergy are specified as mandated reporters:
  Privilege limited to "pastoral communications": Alabama, Arizona, Arkansas, California, Colorado, Illinois, Louisiana, Maine, Massachusetts, Michigan, Minnesota, Missouri, Montana, Nevada, New Mexico, North Dakota, Oregon, Pennsylvania, South Carolina, Vermont, Wisconsin.

  Privilege denied in cases of suspected child abuse or neglect: New Hampshire, West Virginia.

  Privilege not addressed in the reporting laws: Connecticut, Mississippi.

States in which clergy are not specified as mandated reporters but may be included under an "any person" designation:
  Privilege limited to "pastoral communications": Delaware, Florida, Idaho, Kentucky, Maryland, Utah, Wyoming.

  Privilege denied in cases of suspected child abuse or neglect: North Carolina, Rhode Island, Texas.

  Privilege not addressed in the reporting laws: Indiana, Nebraska, New Jersey, Oklahoma, Tennessee, Puerto Rico.

Neither clergy nor "any person" are specified as mandated reporters:
  Privilege limited to "pastoral communications": Washington (Not mandated but if they elect to report, their report and any testimony are provided statutory immunity from liability.)

  Privilege not addressed in the reporting laws: Alaska, American Samoa, District of Columbia, Georgia, Guam, Hawaii, Iowa, Kansas, New York, Northern Mariana Islands, Ohio, South Dakota, Virgin Islands, Virginia.

This information is available in pdf chart form at the Department of Health and Human Services Web site at nccanch.acf.hhs.gov/general/legal/statutes/clergymandated.pdf.

Appendix K

Immunity for Reporters of Child Abuse and Neglect

Under the Child Abuse Prevention and Treatment Act (CAPTA), in order to receive a federal grant, states must make provisions for immunity from prosecution under state and local laws and regulations for individuals making good faith reports of suspected or known instances of child abuse or neglect.[1]

In the United States, every state, the District of Columbia, and the U.S. territories of American Samoa, Guam, Northern Mariana Islands, Puerto Rico, and the Virgin Islands provide some form of immunity from liability for persons who in good faith report suspected instances of abuse or neglect under the reporting laws.

Immunity statutes protect reporters from civil or criminal liability that they might otherwise incur. Several states provide immunity not only for the initial report, but also during any judicial proceedings arising from the report.

For a complete listing of state laws on the immunity afforded you in your state, see the document (pdf format) at the Department of Health and Human Services Web site at nccanch.acf.hhs.gov/general/legal/statutes/immunity.pdf.

Endnotes

Chapter 1:
Coming Soon to Your Church: A Child Molester

1. Don Lattin, "Pedophilia: History Repeats Itself: Abuse Scandal Has Rocked Catholic Church for Years," *San Francisco Chronicle*, 16 June 2002, D-3.
2. "Corrections and Observations About Pedophilia," *Washington Times*, 12 January 2003.
3. A convicted child molester in a large church had been a deacon and a long-time Sunday school teacher, was married with children, and possessed a sterling reputation for "good works" in the church. At his sentencing, a relative (who was then a grown woman) testified that the man had repeatedly molested her when she'd stayed over at his house with his daughter from time to time as a young girl. Another woman testified that, every Sunday, this man would drop all the riders on the bus off except her, then he would pull over to the side of the road and molest her.
4. R. A. Prentky, A. F. S. Lee, R. A. Knight, and D. Cerce draw attention to the fact that the risk of sex offenders recidivating persists long after their discharge from treatment, in some cases fifteen to twenty years later. "Recidivism Rates Among Child Molesters and Rapists: A Methodological Analysis," *Law and*

Human Behavior 21.6: 635–59). Cited in Júlio César Fontana-Rosa, "Legal Competency in a Case of Pedophilia: Advertising on the Internet," *International Journal of Offender Therapy and Comparative Criminology* 45.1 (February 2001): 123.

5. Neil Gilbert, ed., *Combating Child Abuse: International Perspectives and Trends* (New York: Oxford University Press, 1997), 20. The data is drawn from a 1990 survey by Richard Barth, Jill Duerr Berrick, Mark Courtney, and Sylvia Pizzini.

6. George A. Gellert, *Confronting Violence: Answers to Questions about the Epidemic Destroying America's Homes and Communities* (Boulder, Colo.: Westview, 1997), 47.

7. "Law and Disorder: An Interview with Richard Hammar," *Christianity Today* 47.5 (May 2003): 48. See at christianitytoday.com/ct/2003/005/6.48.

8. As noted, it is estimated that the average molester attacks thirteen people before an arrest is made. Amitai Etzioni, "Pedophilia Not Curable, Data Show," *The Atlanta Journal-Constitution,* 21 May 2002, A-21.

9. Gellert, *Confronting Violence,* 47.

10. Ross Macmillan, "Violence and the Life Course: The Consequences of Victimization for Personal and Social Development," *Annual Review of Sociology,* 1 January 2001, 1. See at static.highbeam.com/a/annualreviewofsociology/january012001violenceandthelifecoursetheconsequencesofvictimiza/.

11. U.S. Department of Justice, *Criminal Offender Statistics,* ojp.usdoj.gov/bjs/crimoff.

12. Timothy J. Daily, "Homosexuality and Child Sexual Abuse," *Family Research Council Newsletter* 247 (23 September 2004). See at frc.org/get.cfm?I=IS02E3.

13. Ibid.

14. U.S. Department of Justice, *Criminal Offender Statistics,* ojp.usdoj.gov/bjs/crimoff.

15. Bureau of Justice Statistics, "Sexual Assault of Young Children as Reported to Law Enforcement: Victim, Incident, and Offender Characteristics," *NIBRS Statistical Report,* ojp.usdoj.gov/

bjs/abstract/saycrle. *NIBRS* refers to the National Incident-Based Reporting System.

16. David M. Wagner, quoted in "Corrections and Observations About Pedophilia."

17. Will and Ariel Durant, *The Story of Civilization: The Age of Napoleon* (New York: Simon and Schuster, 1975), 2:91.

Chapter 2:
Appreciating the Danger Posed by Child Molesters

1. On May 17, 1996, U.S. President William Clinton signed Megan's Law into federal law (42 U.S.C. 14071(d)). Now, local law enforcement agencies in all states "shall release relevant information that is necessary to protect the public concerning a specific person required to register under this section."

2. Although the statute was attacked as unconstitutional, it was upheld, and the United States Supreme Court has refused to intervene. All states have enacted a version of Megan's Law, designed to conform to the mandates of the federal statute, in order to protect the public against sex offenders who are required, under state law, to be registered.

3. Beginning in 1994, the United States Congress enacted three statutes that collectively require states to establish or strengthen programs to keep track of sex offenders. The Jacob Wetterling Crimes Against Children and Sexually Violent Offender Registration Act requires states to register sex offenders to alert law enforcement of their presence in the community. The Pam Lychner Sexual Offender Tracking and Identification Act requires states to implement programs designed to notify the public when convicted sex offenders are released into their communities. The Lychner Act also mandates the creation of a national sex offender registry. See sexoffender.com.

4. See chapter 1, note 4.

5. Some experts believe that child molesters are unable to control and adapt themselves to a legal standard of behavior and have

no awareness of the harm done to their victims. See discussion in Júlio César Fontana-Rosa, "Legal Competency in a Case of Pedophilia: Advertising on the Internet," *International Journal of Offender Therapy and Comparative Criminology* 45.1 (February 2001).

6. Amitai Etzioni, a professor of sociology at George Washington University wrote, "The sad truth is that pedophilia is almost never cured. I spent a year reviewing the data on numerous attempts to treat this illness. I turned to study the matter when civil libertarians demanded the repeal of Megan's Law, which requires notification of communities into which pedophiles are released. Such notifications are said to be justified precisely because pedophiles are much more likely than other criminals to be repeat offenders." Amitai Etzioni, "Pedophilia Not Curable, Data Show," *The Atlanta Journal-Constitution,* 21 May 2002, A-21.

7. David Grimm, as quoted in Robyn Suriano, "Medical Experts Struggle to Pinpoint Cause of Pedophilia," *Knight Ridder/ Tribune News Service,* 15 April 2002.

8. Offenders are given injections of Depo-Provera. This drug reduces testosterone levels, which in turn reduces sex drive. There has been much litigation about this treatment. The United States Supreme Court has upheld a state's right to administer the drug against arguments that it is "cruel and unusual" punishment. For an excellent summary of the issues see csun.edu/~psy453/ crimes_n, and read the case *Kansas v. Hendricks,* 521 US 346 (1997).

9. Ernie Allen and Nadine Strossen, "Megan's Law and the Protection of the Child in the On-Line Age," *American Criminal Law Review* 35.4 (1998): 1319.

10. King, Cynthia A., "Fighting the Devil We Don't Know: *Kansas v. Hendricks,* A Case Study Exploring the Civilization of Criminal Punishment and Its Ineffectiveness in Preventing Child Sexual Abuse," *William and Mary Law Review* 40.4 (1999): 1427.

11. *The Butler Eagle,* 16 July 2002. The pastor obtained airline

tickets for the accused molester so that the young man might enroll in a home for troubled young men.

12. Cheryl Wetzstein, "The Child Molestation Dilemma: The World and I," *Washington,* 1 November 1996, 56.

13. Allen and Strossen, "Megan's Law," 1319. Ernie Allen is cofounder, president, and CEO of the National Center for Missing and Exploited Children in Arlington, Virginia. He was director of Public Health and Safety for the city of Louisville, Kentucky, and director of the Louisville–Jefferson County Crime Commission. He has lectured extensively and served on the faculty for the University of Kentucky and other universities.

14. Ibid.

15. California Penal Code § 645 (West, 1997).

16. Christopher Meisenkothen, "Chemical Castration: Breaking the Cycle of Paraphiliac Recidivism," *Social Justice* 26.1 (1999). See at highbeam.com/library/doc0.asp?DOCID=1G1:55541548 &num=1&ctrlInfo=Round8a%3AMode8a%3ASR%3A Result&ao. Reported side effects from Depo-Provera include weight gain, cold sweats, nightmares, muscle weakness, fatigue, breast cancer (in female dogs), and uterine cancer (in monkeys). Others report acne, testicular atrophy, diabetes, hypoglycemia, leg cramps, loss of body hair, insomnia, and phlebitis.

Chapter 3:
A Closer Look at Some Reasons for the Risk

1. David Grimm, as quoted in Robyn Suriano, "Medical Experts Struggle to Pinpoint Cause of Pedophilia," *Knight Ridder/ Tribune News Service,* 15 April 2002.

2. One resource is sexoffender.com, which offers a wide array of background information on individuals. There are other resources, and there may be a local provider. At least, check with your local police department or the local police department in the community where the individual last resided.

3. Dan Burell, letter to author, 3 February 2005.

4. Eighteen-year-old Richard W. Weaverling, a church nursery worker, pleaded guilty to molesting a six-year-old girl, and he received a ten-year suspended sentence in a plea bargain to drop charges that he molested a two-year-old boy. He admitted during court-ordered treatment that he molested every child left in his care. *Washington Post,* 11 November 1995, B.08.

Chapter 4:
Paying Attention to Detail

1. George A. Gellert, *Confronting Violence: Answers to Questions About the Epidemic Destroying America's Homes and Communities* (Boulder, Colo.: Westview, 1997), 60.
2. In this northwest Indiana case, a church deacon and Sunday school teacher was found guilty of the crime and sentenced to eight years in prison. He was released after serving the minimum four years, and was welcomed back into the church with a standing ovation.
3. "Mom: 'No Excuse' for Striking Child," CNN, 23 September 2002. See at archives.cnn.com/2002/US/Midwest/09/23/ tuchman.toogood.cnna/.

Chapter 5:
Safeguards

1. These steps are only suggestions. Some modifications may be appropriate for your church, and some suggestions may not work at all for your circumstances. Review these ideas and take the steps you deem appropriate, given the information at hand.
2. Whether you do this only for male volunteers or for all volunteers is something you have to decide. I'd suggest you do it for everyone. Writing reports has some value beyond the screening process for legal protection. It also emphasizes the importance of the job in the mind of the applicant. It becomes serious busi-

ness. And that is what all of God's work ought to be—*serious business.*

3. See appendix G, "Mandatory Reporters of Child Abuse and Neglect" (United States).
4. See appendix I, "Definitions of Child Abuse and Neglect."
5. See appendix K, "Immunity for Reporters of Child Abuse and Neglect."
6. See appendix J, "Clergy as Mandatory Reporters of Child Abuse and Neglect."
7. Realize you may be preaching to a jury, so get it all in now. That tape may one day be played to a jury by your attorney to show the church's position and the aggressiveness of the church in guarding against predators. It is this lack of aggressiveness and hostility toward those who attack children that is costing the Roman Catholic Church billions of dollars.
8. "South Jersey Deacon Accused of Molesting Boys at Church Sleepover," *Associated Press*, 2 November 2004. See at rickross. com/reference/clergy/clergy335.

Chapter 6:
It Happened: What Is Our Liability?

1. In some locations, such as a drug-infested, high-crime neighborhood, a church might argue that no one is really "safe" in the church. But even if the location was in the worst of neighborhoods, this argument will mean little if the predator was part of the church community or was sanctioned by the church to have some level of access to the victimized child.
2. *ABC News*, 2 November 2002; see also, "Three lawsuits filed against Nebraska church for alleged sexual abuse," Associated Press: *Union Tribune*, 2 November 2002. See at crossword.uniontrib.com/news/nation/20021102-0212-churchschoollawsuits.
3. *Doe v. Samaritan Counseling Center*, 791 P 2d 344 (Alaska 1990).
4. Rob Moll, "Lutheran Church Abuse Victims Receive $69 Million

Settlement," *Christianity Today,* 23 April 2004. See at christianitytoday.com/ct/2004/116/51.0.

5. A church in Florida was sued by a mother when her five-year-old daughter was molested on a church bus by a church volunteer worker who'd served five years for sexual battery on a minor in New York. The complaint charged that church officials had failed to screen his background. The church settled the suit for $20,000. Cary Davis, "Church Is Sued Over Molestation," *St. Petersburg Times,* June 25, 2002, http://sptimes.com/2002/06/25/news_pf/Pasco/Church_is_sued_over_m.shtlm 10 December 2002, 1.

Chapter 7:
Sexual Assaults by Leaders

1. "Church Sued Over Abuse in 1992," *The Seattle Times,* 20 November 2004. See at rickross.com/reference/clergy/clergy341.

2. *Burlington, (N.C.), Alamance County Times-News,* 11 April 2000. See at thetimesnews.com/2000/00-04/00-04-11/news-1.

3. Combs's wife, Evangeline, was also sentenced to prison. They had taken the young girl years before from a Christian home in Indiana and were to have adopted her but never got around to formalizing the adoption. Combs moved to Tennessee, where he became a pastor.

4. *Grants Pass (Ore.) Daily Courier,* 17 April 1992.

5. *Abilene (Tex.) Reporter-News,* 18 October 2002.

6. *Duluth (Minn.) News-Tribune,* 25 September 1994; 28 February 1995.

7. *Cedar Rapids (Iowa) Gazette,* 30 March 1995.

8. *Tulsa World,* 16 June 1995; 17 June 1995.

9. *Tulsa World,* 27 May 1995.

10. *Duluth (Minn.) News-Tribune,* 23 May 1995. For a view of the appellate court's decision, see reformation.com/CSA/reeb1.

11. *Lexington (Ky.) Herald-Leader,* 31 October 1995; 4 November 1995.

12. *San Jose (Calif.) Mercury News,* 4 April 1995.
13. *Indianapolis Star,* 28 January 1993; Indiana Sex Offender Registry for Wabash County, cheetaa.com/wabashcountyregistry.
14. Jonathan Hart was convicted in Eastland, Texas, February 1999, on three counts of sexual assault of a minor child. A civil suit was filed naming the United Pentecostal Church International (UPCI) in Saint Louis, Missouri, the Texas District of the United Pentecostal Church, the United Pentecostal Church of Eastland, Texas, Bobby Hart (the father) and Jonathan Mark Hart. For a detailed account, see: reformation.com/CSA/Hart1.
15. In the U.S., much of this will depend on state laws. Knowledge of a crime by a church official is almost certain to expose the church and the official(s) to legal liability.
16. This is one reason why, in this author's opinion, a church should never be "pastor ruled." Baptist churches are typically *led* by the pastor and a governing board of deacons with ultimate approval by the congregation. Presbyterian government is representative, with the congregation electing elders and deacons. Episcopal churches have authority controlled at the district level. In practice, however, the senior pastor of a congregation can come to exert an unhealthy level of control, whatever the form of government. The real concern should be that the fate of the church never rest in the control and domination of a single individual. That is a recipe for disaster, because it invites a man to rule without accountability.

Chapter 8:
A Duty to Report?

1. See appendix G, "Mandatory Reporters of Child Abuse and Neglect (United States)." This comprehensive list of state laws provides an excellent overview of who is or is not required to report. The information is compiled by the federal government through the National Clearinghouse on Child Abuse and

Neglect, which is a part of the U.S. Department of Health and Human Services.

2. Howard Davidson, "Failure to Report Child Abuse: Legal Penalties and Emerging Issues," *Professional Responsibilities in Protecting Children: A Public Health Approach to Child Sexual Abuse*, edited by Ann Maney and Susan Wells (New York: Praeger Publishers, 1988), 93.

3. See appendix H, "Penalties for Failure to Report (United States)." This information is compiled by the federal government through the National Clearinghouse on Child Abuse and Neglect Information, part of the U.S. Department of Health and Human Services. The complete information is at nccanch. acf.hhs.gov/general/legal/statutes/report.pdf.

4. "Confessional Seal Under Attack in Several States," *America* 188.10 (24 March 2003). See at americamagazing.org/ gettext.cfm?articleTypeID=29&textID=2864&issueID=427. This battle is reported in detail by the Catholic News Service. See catholicnews.com. See, also, appendix J, "Clergy as Mandatory Reporters of Child Abuse and Neglect." Some clergy may have no choice but to speak up. At this writing, new laws appear to be turning in that direction. In much of the U.S., clergy-penitent privilege in child abuse cases has been narrowed or even eliminated.

5. Walter A. Elwell, ed., *Topical Analysis of the Bible* (Grand Rapids: Baker, 1991).

6. Jay E. Adams, *Handbook of Church Discipline* (Grand Rapids: Zondervan, 1986).

7. This will not set well with some, but it keeps a minister from having to wrestle about whether to violate a confidence when he holds information about a crime and is bound by an oath of secrecy.

8. Ronald K. Bullis and Cynthia S. Mazur, *Legal Issues and Religious Counseling*, 1st ed. (Louisville: Westminster–John Knox, 1993), 113.

9. *Portsmouth* (New Hampshire) *Herald,* 22 September 2002.
10. Maney and Wells, eds., *Professional Responsibilities,* 101.

Chapter 9:
Insurance Coverage

1. Ross Eatman, "10 Civil Damages Suits Against Professionals in Cases of Child Sexual Abuse," in *Professional Responsibilities in Protecting Children: A Public Health Approach to Child Sexual Abuse,* edited by Ann Maney and Susan Wells (New York: Praeger Publishers, 1988), 110.
2. Caroline McDonald, "Sexual Abuse Coverage Can Be Found (Liability)," *National Underwriter Property and Casualty/Risk and Benefits Management* 106.40 (7 October 2002): 18–19.
3. Ibid.
4. Perry A. Zirkel, "Insurance Liability: Don't Make an Error About an Omission," *Phi Delta Kappan* 78.8 (April 1997): 658.
5. Church Mutual Insurance Company, Safeco, Brotherhood Mutual Insurance Company, and Guide One Insurance are four companies with extensive experience in church insurance coverage.

Appendix G:
Mandatory Reporters of Child Abuse and Neglect (United States)

1. This summary is adapted from the Child Abuse and Neglect State Statutes Series, which is produced by the National Clearinghouse on Child Abuse and Neglect Information. The Clearinghouse is a service of the Children's Bureau, Administration for Children and Families, U.S. Department of Health and Human Services. Used by permission.

   The Statutes-at-a-Glance series highlights specific topics from the Child Abuse and Neglect State Statutes Compendium of Laws, presented in a table format to provide quick comparisons of statutory provisions across the United States. The Compendium is a compilation of state laws on different topics related to child maltreatment reporting laws, central registries, permanency planning, and domestic violence. For a complete listing of individuals mandated to report suspected child maltreatment, see the Department of Health and Human Services Web site at nccanch.acf.hhs .gov/general/legal/statutes/manda.cfm.

2. The word *approximately* is used to emphasize that statutes are constantly being revised and updated.

3. Privileged communications may be addressed in other sections of a state's law, typically in rules of evidence or civil procedure.

Appendix H:
Reporting Penalties

1. This summary is adapted from the Child Abuse and Neglect State Statutes Series, which is produced by the National Clearinghouse on Child Abuse and Neglect Information. The Clearinghouse is a service of the Children's Bureau, Administration for Children and Families, U.S. Department of Health and Human Services. See Appendix G, note 1.

2. The word *approximately* is used to emphasize that statutes are constantly being revised and updated.

Appendix I:
Definitions of Child Abuse and Neglect

1. This summary is adapted from the Child Abuse and Neglect State Statutes Series, which is produced by the National Clearinghouse on Child Abuse and Neglect Information. The Clearinghouse is a service of the Children's Bureau, Administration for Children and Families, U.S. Department of Health and Human Services. Used by permission. See Appendix G, note 1.

Appendix J:
Clergy as Mandatory Reporters of
Child Abuse and Neglect

1. This summary is adapted from the Child Abuse and Neglect State Statutes Series, which is produced by the National Clearinghouse on Child Abuse and Neglect Information. The Clearinghouse is a service of the Children's Bureau, Administration for Children and Families, U.S. Department of Health and Human Services. Used by permission. See Appendix G, note 1.

Appendix K:
Immunity for Reporters of
Child Abuse and Neglect

1. This summary is adapted from the Child Abuse and Neglect State Statutes Series, which is produced by the National Clearinghouse on Child Abuse and Neglect Information. The Clearinghouse is a service of the Children's Bureau, Administration for Children and Families, U.S. Department of Health and Human Services. Used by permission. See Appendix G, note 1.

Also from Kregel Academic and Professional

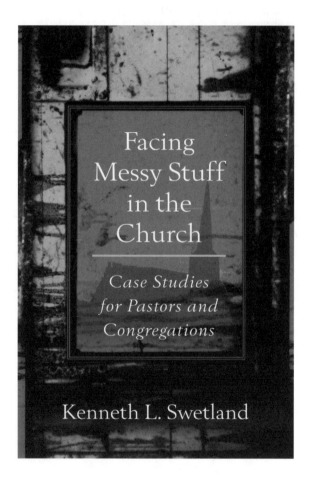

"Pastors are on the front line facing an array of human problems. One pastor I know refers to his daily ministry as 'facing messy stuff.' This book contains case studies that reflect a variety of the 'messy stuff' that churches and pastors face in the normal course of being the church in the world."
—From the preface

0-8254-3696-6 • 224 pages • Paperback

Also from Kregel Academic and Professional

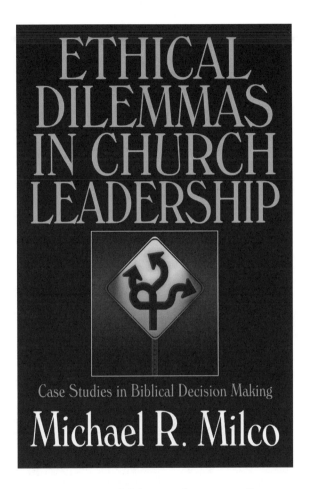

Child abuse . . . AIDS . . . infidelity . . . homosexuality . . . unexpected pregnancies.

These social problems are widespread —and churches are not immune. Author Michael R. Milco shares case studies on some of the most sensitive issues pastors and church leaders face and how to apply biblical principles to the problem-solving process.

0-8254-3197-2 • 192 pages • Paperback